BIRTHDAY
DICTIONARY

BIRTHDAY
DICTIONARY

EVERYTHING YOU NEED TO KNOW
TO FIND THE KEY TO YOUR INNER
NATURE AND PERSONALITY

COMPREHENSIVE EXPLANATIONS
OF THE ZODIAC, FLOWERS, GEMSTONES,
COLORS, AND NUMBERS RELATING
TO EACH BIRTH DATE

Antonia Beattie

THUNDER BAY
P · R · E · S · S

San Diego, California

Because the birthday of my life
Is come, my love is come to me.

CHRISTINA ROSSETTI

CONTENTS

INTRODUCTION

Your birthday is the key to your personality

Self-knowledge can enrich our lives. "Know thyself," declared the Oracle at Delphi when the ancient Greeks sought advice for future happiness. Since time immemorial, people have been seeking enlightenment from the world around them. This quest has revealed many useful sources. As you will see in this book, the planets have taught the rich secrets of Western and Chinese astrology, and nature has revealed its secrets also in systems such as Native American astrology. In Western astrology, the position of the sun when you were born is believed to influence your personality, affecting your potential for success, creativity, and happiness in various areas of life. The sun, a life-giving force, is often associated with creativity, talent and chances of success in business and other aspects of life.

Numerology, the study of numbers, has enabled many to penetrate the mysteries of life. The Ancients put great store in the powerful vibrations of numbers. In ancient Greece, about 2,500 years ago, Pythagoras wrote of the qualities and relative relationships of each of the nine numbers, which he believed to be profoundly mystical.

Meaning has also been drawn from the elements of nature. The earth itself, with its colors, its herbs and flowers, and its gemstones, has much to tell.

You will find this dictionary a comprehensive repository of the knowledge referred to above. This will enable you to meet the continuing challenge to understand yourself better. You will learn about the implications of many aspects of your birthday: the hour, month, season, and year of birth, as well as the planetary aspects ruling at that time. Learning about them will give you more insights into yourself and your place in a complex, often confusing, modern world.

For the ancient Chinese, astrology was a complicated system that could help predict the outcome of many relationships. In this system, the date and the time of birth govern an array of unique personality types, none of which is considered "better" than another. The same applies to all other systems of astrology examined in this book. Each of the types described represents a beneficial approach to life. Wisdom is said to be in the hands of those who understand this and apply appropriate behavior and flexibility in their communication style.

In the ancient system of animal totem astrology practiced by Native Americans in the past and today, the birthday is highly significant. The animal totem is an animal, fish, or bird that represents a particular time of birth and season of birth, as well as allied elements of nature. Knowing about your animal totem can give you insight into yourself. In times of trouble, associating yourself with the animal totems of other people will allow you to take on the characteristics of others and understand more about yourself.

Please note that for most systems, some variations exist. For example, some Native American tribes have differing totems for time of birth, the seasons, and/or the elements. This book presents the more widely known animal totems. Dates may vary in the Western zodiac system. There are also some variant animal names in Chinese astrology.

You, your friends, and your family—whoever delves into this volume—will both delight in and profit from exploring the centuries of accumulated knowledge it offers. This dictionary will also help you to:

- Prepare your own birthday profile and that of others, and interpret the meaning of each profile.
- Identify the strengths and weaknesses in a given profile and learn how to work with them.
- Make more appropriate choices in all areas of life, from career to friendships and other relationships.

How to use this dictionary

The hour, day, month, and year of your birth give a great deal of information about your inner personality and what influences your destiny. They can also provide you with information about what colors, foods, flowers, herbs, gemstones, and numbers are lucky or beneficial for you.

1. HOUR OF BIRTH

The first step to using this dictionary is to turn to "Your birthday at a glance," pages 10–39. The table on page 11 reveals the importance of the hour in which you were born. According to Chinese astrology, the hour of your birth corresponds to one of twelve symbolic animals that can reveal aspects of your hidden self.

Once you know which animal corresponds with your time of birth, see the A–Z section (from page 48) for what this means in terms of your secret or inner life. For example, if you were born between 3 A.M. and 5 A.M., your time period corresponds to the tiger. You can read about the tiger on pages 166–167.

2. DATE OF BIRTH

Next, turn to the day of birth table on pages 12–31. This table lists, for every day of the year, what the day of birth means in terms of astrological signs in both traditional Western and the Native American zodiacs. Every day of the year is listed, and the table also outlines some of the corresponding colors, foods, flowers, herbs, and gemstones. See also pages 36–39 for a more detailed list of birth colors, flowers, herbs, and gemstones.

This book offers a special feature—a comprehensive template you can use to create a detailed personalized chart of what your birthday means to you (see pages 40-45). You can photocopy this template and use it for yourself, your family, and your friends. Record on it all that you find out about the meaning of the various aspects of your birthday and keep it as a handy reference.

EXAMPLE: IN THE NORTHERN HEMISPHERE

Day	27
Month	March
Western zodiac	Aries
Western element	Fire
Native American	Hawk
Native American element	Fire
Color	Red
Food	Blackberry
Flower	Daffodil
Herb	Garlic, chili
Gemstone	Garnet, diamond

3. SIGNS OF THE ZODIAC

You will find the zodiac signs in the traditional Western and Native American zodiacs in the A–Z section. The corresponding elements, such as fire, are also listed alphabetically in this section. Use the information given here to supplement your insights.

4. OTHER ITEMS

In various astrological systems, there are specific minerals, semiprecious stones and plants associated with each sign of the zodiac or animal sign. See pages 36–39, for a detailed list of birth colors, flowers, herbs, and gemstones.

5. PERSONALITY AND LOVE LIFE

Enjoy the revelations concerning your personality and love life within these tables.

6. MORE DETAILED INFORMATION

Once you have accessed the tables, more detailed information can be garnered from the A–Z section. Enjoy using this dictionary for exploration and revelation.

7. COLOR KEY

A color key has been used in the A–Z section to help you easily identify the astrological system listed.

● CHINESE ASTROLOGY   ● NATIVE AMERICAN

● WESTERN ASTROLOGY   ● NUMEROLOGY

Your birthday by the hour

In Chinese astrology, the hour, month, and year of your birth all contribute to defining your personality. Each person has two animal signs—a dominant sign and an ascendant sign. The dominant sign is the animal ruling over your *year* of birth (see pages 31–33). This animal sign determines your personality structure. The ascendant sign is the animal sign ruling over your *time* of birth (see table opposite). The personality traits associated with this sign modify the personality structure determined by your dominant sign. The ascendant sign indicates your hidden self. This is the way you perceive yourself and is the side you conceal from others.

The ancient Chinese saw the day as two-hourly segments, each ruled by one of the animal signs. If you know what time of day you were born, you can find your hourly sign in the table at right. If you were born during daylight saving time, you will need to deduct one hour from your time of birth. If you are not sure under which of two signs your birthday falls, read about both signs. A pure sign occurs when the dominant and ascendant signs are the same.

TIME OF BIRTH: ASCENDANT SIGN, YOUR HIDDEN SELF		
HOUR	ANIMAL	ATTRIBUTES
11 P.M. to 1 A.M.	Rat	The Rat as the ascendant sign stimulates the mental aspects of the personality and boosts both social charms and communication skills.
1 A.M. to 3 A.M.	Ox	The Ox as the ascendant sign adds practicality, determination, and physical energy to the personality, as well as an appreciation of sensual pleasures.
3 A.M. to 5 A.M.	Tiger	The Tiger as the ascendant sign will endow the personality with passion, courage, and conviction. Those with this sign as the ascendant will also find hidden strengths within themselves when dealing with loss or ill health.
5 A.M. to 7 A.M.	Rabbit	The Rabbit as the ascendant sign will add flexibility and balance to the personality. Rabbit ascendants are peace lovers and tactful when dealing with others.
7 A.M. to 9 A.M.	Dragon	When the Dragon is the ascendant sign, its influence will create a magnetic personality. Those with a Dragon ascendant usually display independence and confidence.
9 A.M. to 11 A.M.	Snake	Having the Snake as the ascendant sign gives rise to reflection on the self, objectivity, and wisdom. Snakes radiate sexuality and attractiveness.
11 A.M. to 1 P.M.	Horse	The Horse as the ascendant sign adds vitality and physical agility to the personality. Those with Horse ascendants also become restless and bored easily.
1 P.M. to 3 P.M.	Sheep	Having the Sheep as the ascendant sign will add peace and serenity to the personality. People with this ascendant sign may be flexible and light-hearted.
3 P.M. to 5 P.M.	Monkey	The Monkey as the ascendant sign will add mental agility to the personality. Monkeys may also have a keen wit and be skilled at comedy.
5 P.M. to 7 P.M.	Rooster	The Rooster as the ascendant sign ensures integrity and a sense of honor. Those with the Rooster as their ascendant are keenly alert and quick to voice their opinions.
7 P.M. to 9 P.M.	Dog	This ascendant sign imparts an ethical, principled nature. Those with the Dog as the ascendant sign are loyal and just in their dealings with others.
9 P.M. to 11 P.M.	Pig	Having the Pig as the ascendant sign means a carefree attitude to life and a focus on enjoyment and self-indulgence.

Your birthday by the day

	DAY	WESTERN ZODIAC	NATIVE AMERICAN BIRTH TIME ANIMAL	NATIVE AMERICAN SEASONAL ELEMENT
JANUARY	1	Capricorn	N*: Snow goose S: Woodpecker	N: Air S: Water
	2	Capricorn	N: Snow goose S: Woodpecker	N: Air S: Water
	3	Capricorn	N: Snow goose S: Woodpecker	N: Air S: Water
	4	Capricorn	N: Snow goose S: Woodpecker	N: Air S: Water
	5	Capricorn	N: Snow goose S: Woodpecker	N: Air S: Water
	6	Capricorn	N: Snow goose S: Woodpecker	N: Air S: Water
	7	Capricorn	N: Snow goose S: Woodpecker	N: Air S: Water
	8	Capricorn	N: Snow goose S: Woodpecker	N: Air S: Water
	9	Capricorn	N: Snow goose S: Woodpecker	N: Air S: Water
	10	Capricorn	N: Snow goose S: Woodpecker	N: Air S: Water
	11	Capricorn	N: Snow goose S: Woodpecker	N: Air S: Water
	12	Capricorn	N: Snow goose S: Woodpecker	N: Air S: Water
	13	Capricorn	N: Snow goose S: Woodpecker	N: Air S: Water
	14	Capricorn	N: Snow goose S: Woodpecker	N: Air S: Water
	15	Capricorn	N: Snow goose S: Woodpecker	N: Air S: Water
	16	Capricorn	N: Snow goose S: Woodpecker	N: Air S: Water
	17	Capricorn	N: Snow goose S: Woodpecker	N: Air S: Water
	18	Capricorn	N: Snow goose S: Woodpecker	N: Air S: Water
	19	Capricorn	N: Snow goose S: Woodpecker	N: Air S: Water
	20	Capricorn	N: Otter S: Salmon	N: Air S: Water
	21	Capricorn	N: Otter S: Salmon	N: Air S: Water
	22	Aquarius	N: Otter S: Salmon	N: Air S: Water
	23	Aquarius	N: Otter S: Salmon	N: Air S: Water
	24	Aquarius	N: Otter S: Salmon	N: Air S: Water
	25	Aquarius	N: Otter S: Salmon	N: Air S: Water
	26	Aquarius	N: Otter S: Salmon	N: Air S: Water
	27	Aquarius	N: Otter S: Salmon	N: Air S: Water
	28	Aquarius	N: Otter S: Salmon	N: Air S: Water
	29	Aquarius	N: Otter S: Salmon	N: Air S: Water
	30	Aquarius	N: Otter S: Salmon	N: Air S: Water
	31	Aquarius	N: Otter S: Salmon	N: Air S: Water
FEBRUARY	1	Aquarius	N: Otter S: Salmon	N: Air S: Water
	2	Aquarius	N: Otter S: Salmon	N: Air S: Water
	3	Aquarius	N: Otter S: Salmon	N: Air S: Water
	4	Aquarius	N: Otter S: Salmon	N: Air S: Water
	5	Aquarius	N: Otter S: Salmon	N: Air S: Water
	6	Aquarius	N: Otter S: Salmon	N: Air S: Water
	7	Aquarius	N: Otter S: Salmon	N: Air S: Water
	8	Aquarius	N: Otter S: Salmon	N: Air S: Water
	9	Aquarius	N: Otter S: Salmon	N: Air S: Water
	10	Aquarius	N: Otter S: Salmon	N: Air S: Water
	11	Aquarius	N: Otter S: Salmon	N: Air S: Water
	12	Aquarius	N: Otter S: Salmon	N: Air S: Water

* N = NORTHERN HEMISPHERE, S = SOUTHERN HEMISPHERE

COLOR	FLOWERS	HERBS	GEMSTONES
Green	Carnation	Comfrey	Garnet
Green	Carnation	Comfrey	Garnet
Green	Carnation	Comfrey	Garnet
Green	Carnation	Comfrey	Garnet
Green	Carnation	Comfrey	Garnet
Green	Carnation	Comfrey	Garnet
Green	Carnation	Comfrey	Garnet
Green	Carnation	Comfrey	Garnet
Green	Carnation	Comfrey	Garnet
Green	Carnation	Comfrey	Garnet
Green	Carnation	Comfrey	Garnet
Green	Carnation	Comfrey	Garnet
Green	Carnation	Comfrey	Garnet
Green	Carnation	Comfrey	Garnet
Green	Carnation	Comfrey	Garnet
Green	Carnation	Comfrey	Garnet
Green	Carnation	Comfrey	Garnet
Green	Carnation	Comfrey	Garnet
Green	Carnation	Comfrey	Garnet
Green	Carnation	Comfrey	Garnet
Green	Carnation	Comfrey	Garnet
Royal blue	Carnation	Elder flower	Amethyst
Royal blue	Carnation	Elder flower	Amethyst
Royal blue	Carnation	Elder flower	Amethyst
Royal blue	Carnation	Elder flower	Amethyst
Royal blue	Carnation	Elder flower	Amethyst
Royal blue	Carnation	Elder flower	Amethyst
Royal blue	Carnation	Elder flower	Amethyst
Royal blue	Carnation	Elder flower	Amethyst
Royal blue	Carnation	Elder flower	Amethyst
Royal blue	Carnation	Elder flower	Amethyst
Royal blue	Violet	Elder flower	Amethyst
Royal blue	Violet	Elder flower	Amethyst
Royal blue	Violet	Elder flower	Amethyst
Royal blue	Violet	Elder flower	Amethyst
Royal blue	Violet	Elder flower	Amethyst
Royal blue	Violet	Elder flower	Amethyst
Royal blue	Violet	Elder flower	Amethyst
Royal blue	Violet	Elder flower	Amethyst
Royal blue	Violet	Elder flower	Amethyst
Royal blue	Violet	Elder flower	Amethyst
Royal blue	Violet	Elder flower	Amethyst
Royal blue	Violet	Elder flower	Amethyst

	DAY	WESTERN ZODIAC	NATIVE AMERICAN BIRTH TIME ANIMAL	NATIVE AMERICAN SEASONAL ELEMENT
FEBRUARY	13	Aquarius	N: Otter S: Salmon	N: Air S: Water
	14	Aquarius	N: Otter S: Salmon	N: Air S: Water
	15	Aquarius	N: Otter S: Salmon	N: Air S: Water
	16	Aquarius	N: Otter S: Salmon	N: Air S: Water
	17	Aquarius	N: Otter S: Salmon	N: Air S: Water
	18	Aquarius	N: Otter S: Salmon	N: Air S: Water
	19	Aquarius	N: Wolf S: Brown bear	N: Air S: Water
	20	Aquarius	N: Wolf S: Brown bear	N: Air S: Water
	21	Pisces	N: Wolf S: Brown bear	N: Air S: Water
	22	Pisces	N: Wolf S: Brown bear	N: Air S: Water
	23	Pisces	N: Wolf S: Brown bear	N: Air S: Water
	24	Pisces	N: Wolf S: Brown bear	N: Air S: Water
	25	Pisces	N: Wolf S: Brown bear	N: Air S: Water
	26	Pisces	N: Wolf S: Brown bear	N: Air S: Water
	27	Pisces	N: Wolf S: Brown bear	N: Air S: Water
	28	Pisces	N: Wolf S: Brown bear	N: Air S: Water
	29	Pisces	N: Wolf S: Brown bear	N: Air S: Water
MARCH	1	Pisces	N: Wolf S: Brown bear	N: Air S: Water
	2	Pisces	N: Wolf S: Brown bear	N: Air S: Water
	3	Pisces	N: Wolf S: Brown bear	N: Air S: Water
	4	Pisces	N: Wolf S: Brown bear	N: Air S: Water
	5	Pisces	N: Wolf S: Brown bear	N: Air S: Water
	6	Pisces	N: Wolf S: Brown bear	N: Air S: Water
	7	Pisces	N: Wolf S: Brown bear	N: Air S: Water
	8	Pisces	N: Wolf S: Brown bear	N: Air S: Water
	9	Pisces	N: Wolf S: Brown bear	N: Air S: Water
	10	Pisces	N: Wolf S: Brown bear	N: Air S: Water
	11	Pisces	N: Wolf S: Brown bear	N: Air S: Water
	12	Pisces	N: Wolf S: Brown bear	N: Air S: Water
	13	Pisces	N: Wolf S: Brown bear	N: Air S: Water
	14	Pisces	N: Wolf S: Brown bear	N: Air S: Water
	15	Pisces	N: Wolf S: Brown bear	N: Air S: Water
	16	Pisces	N: Otter S: Brown bear	N: Air S: Water
	17	Pisces	N: Wolf S: Brown bear	N: Air S: Water
	18	Pisces	N: Wolf S: Brown bear	N: Air S: Water
	19	Pisces	N: Wolf S: Brown bear	N: Air S: Water
	20	Aries	N: Wolf S: Brown bear	N: Air S: Water
	21	Aries	N: Hawk S: Raven	N: Fire S: Earth
	22	Aries	N: Hawk S: Raven	N: Fire S: Earth
	23	Aries	N: Hawk S: Raven	N: Fire S: Earth
	24	Aries	N: Hawk S: Raven	N: Fire S: Earth
	25	Aries	N: Hawk S: Raven	N: Fire S: Earth
	26	Aries	N: Hawk S: Raven	N: Fire S: Earth
	27	Aries	N: Hawk S: Raven	N: Fire S: Earth
	28	Aries	N: Hawk S: Raven	N: Fire S: Earth
	29	Aries	N: Hawk S: Raven	N: Fire S: Earth

COLOR	FLOWERS	HERBS	GEMSTONES
Royal blue	Violet	Elder flower	Amethyst
Royal blue	Violet	Elder flower	Amethyst
Royal blue	Violet	Elder flower	Amethyst
Royal blue	Violet	Elder flower	Amethyst
Royal blue	Violet	Elder flower	Amethyst
Royal blue	Violet	Elder flower	Amethyst
Royal blue	Violet	Elder flower	Amethyst
Royal blue	Violet	Elder flower	Amethyst
Aquamarine	Violet	Rose hip	Aquamarine
Aquamarine	Violet	Rose hip	Aquamarine
Aquamarine	Violet	Rose hip	Aquamarine
Aquamarine	Violet	Rose hip	Aquamarine
Aquamarine	Violet	Rose hip	Aquamarine
Aquamarine	Violet	Rose hip	Aquamarine
Aquamarine	Violet	Rose hip	Aquamarine
Aquamarine	Violet	Rose hip	Aquamarine
Aquamarine	Violet	Rose hip	Aquamarine
Aquamarine	Daffodil	Rose hip	Aquamarine
Aquamarine	Daffodil	Rose hip	Aquamarine
Aquamarine	Daffodil	Rose hip	Aquamarine
Aquamarine	Daffodil	Rose hip	Aquamarine
Aquamarine	Daffodil	Rose hip	Aquamarine
Aquamarine	Daffodil	Rose hip	Aquamarine
Aquamarine	Daffodil	Rose hip	Aquamarine
Aquamarine	Daffodil	Rose hip	Aquamarine
Aquamarine	Daffodil	Rose hip	Aquamarine
Aquamarine	Daffodil	Rose hip	Aquamarine
Aquamarine	Daffodil	Rose hip	Aquamarine
Aquamarine	Daffodil	Rose hip	Aquamarine
Aquamarine	Daffodil	Rose hip	Aquamarine
Aquamarine	Daffodil	Rose hip	Aquamarine
Aquamarine	Daffodil	Rose hip	Aquamarine
Aquamarine	Daffodil	Rose hip	Aquamarine
Aquamarine	Daffodil	Rose hip	Aquamarine
Aquamarine	Daffodil	Rose hip	Aquamarine
Red	Daffodil	Garlic	Diamond
Red	Daffodil	Garlic	Diamond
Red	Daffodil	Garlic	Diamond
Red	Daffodil	Garlic	Diamond
Red	Daffodil	Garlic	Diamond
Red	Daffodil	Garlic	Diamond
Red	Daffodil	Garlic	Diamond
Red	Daffodil	Garlic	Diamond
Red	Daffodil	Garlic	Diamond
Red	Daffodil	Garlic	Diamond

▶

DAY	WESTERN ZODIAC	NATIVE AMERICAN BIRTH TIME ANIMAL	NATIVE AMERICAN SEASONAL ELEMENT
30	Aries	N: Hawk S: Raven	N: Fire S: Earth
31	Aries	N: Hawk S: Raven	N: Fire S: Earth
1	Aries	N: Hawk S: Raven	N: Fire S: Earth
2	Aries	N: Hawk S: Raven	N: Fire S: Earth
3	Aries	N: Hawk S: Raven	N: Fire S: Earth
4	Aries	N: Hawk S: Raven	N: Fire S: Earth
5	Aries	N: Hawk S: Raven	N: Fire S: Earth
6	Aries	N: Hawk S: Raven	N: Fire S: Earth
7	Aries	N: Hawk S: Raven	N: Fire S: Earth
8	Aries	N: Hawk S: Raven	N: Fire S: Earth
9	Aries	N: Hawk S: Raven	N: Fire S: Earth
10	Aries	N: Hawk S: Raven	N: Fire S: Earth
11	Aries	N: Hawk S: Raven	N: Fire S: Earth
12	Aries	N: Hawk S: Raven	N: Fire S: Earth
13	Aries	N: Hawk S: Raven	N: Fire S: Earth
14	Aries	N: Hawk S: Raven	N: Fire S: Earth
15	Aries	N: Hawk S: Raven	N: Fire S: Earth
16	Aries	N: Hawk S: Raven	N: Fire S: Earth
17	Aries	N: Hawk S: Raven	N: Fire S: Earth
18	Aries	N: Hawk S: Raven	N: Fire S: Earth
19	Aries	N: Hawk S: Raven	N: Fire S: Earth
20	Aries	N: Beaver S: Snake	N: Fire S: Earth
21	Taurus	N: Beaver S: Snake	N: Fire S: Earth
22	Taurus	N: Beaver S: Snake	N: Fire S: Earth
23	Taurus	N: Beaver S: Snake	N: Fire S: Earth
24	Taurus	N: Beaver S: Snake	N: Fire S: Earth
25	Taurus	N: Beaver S: Snake	N: Fire S: Earth
26	Taurus	N: Beaver S: Snake	N: Fire S: Earth
27	Taurus	N: Beaver S: Snake	N: Fire S: Earth
28	Taurus	N: Beaver S: Snake	N: Fire S: Earth
29	Taurus	N: Beaver S: Snake	N: Fire S: Earth
30	Taurus	N: Beaver S: Snake	N: Fire S: Earth
1	Taurus	N: Beaver S: Snake	N: Fire S: Earth
2	Taurus	N: Beaver S: Snake	N: Fire S: Earth
3	Taurus	N: Beaver S: Snake	N: Fire S: Earth
4	Taurus	N: Beaver S: Snake	N: Fire S: Earth
5	Taurus	N: Beaver S: Snake	N: Fire S: Earth
6	Taurus	N: Beaver S: Snake	N: Fire S: Earth
7	Taurus	N: Beaver S: Snake	N: Fire S: Earth
8	Taurus	N: Beaver S: Snake	N: Fire S: Earth
9	Taurus	N: Beaver S: Snake	N: Fire S: Earth
10	Taurus	N: Beaver S: Snake	N: Fire S: Earth
11	Taurus	N: Beaver S: Snake	N: Fire S: Earth
12	Taurus	N: Beaver S: Snake	N: Fire S: Earth
13	Taurus	N: Beaver S: Snake	N: Fire S: Earth

APRIL

MAY

COLOR	FLOWERS	HERBS	GEMSTONES
Red	Daffodil	Garlic	Diamond
Red	Daffodil	Garlic	Diamond
Red	Sweet pea	Garlic	Diamond
Red	Sweet pea	Garlic	Diamond
Red	Sweet pea	Garlic	Diamond
Red	Sweet pea	Garlic	Diamond
Red	Sweet pea	Garlic	Diamond
Red	Sweet pea	Garlic	Diamond
Red	Sweet pea	Garlic	Diamond
Red	Sweet pea	Garlic	Diamond
Red	Sweet pea	Garlic	Diamond
Red	Sweet pea	Garlic	Diamond
Red	Sweet pea	Garlic	Diamond
Red	Sweet pea	Garlic	Diamond
Red	Sweet pea	Garlic	Diamond
Red	Sweet pea	Garlic	Diamond
Red	Sweet pea	Garlic	Diamond
Red	Sweet pea	Garlic	Diamond
Red	Sweet pea	Garlic	Diamond
Red	Sweet pea	Garlic	Diamond
Red	Sweet pea	Garlic	Diamond
Red	Sweet pea	Garlic	Diamond
Red	Sweet pea	Garlic	Diamond
Pink	Sweet pea	Peppermint	Emerald
Pink	Sweet pea	Peppermint	Emerald
Pink	Sweet pea	Peppermint	Emerald
Pink	Sweet pea	Peppermint	Emerald
Pink	Sweet pea	Peppermint	Emerald
Pink	Sweet pea	Peppermint	Emerald
Pink	Sweet pea	Peppermint	Emerald
Pink	Sweet pea	Peppermint	Emerald
Pink	Sweet pea	Peppermint	Emerald
Pink	Sweet pea	Peppermint	Emerald
Pink	Lily of the valley	Peppermint	Emerald
Pink	Lily of the valley	Peppermint	Emerald
Pink	Lily of the valley	Peppermint	Emerald
Pink	Lily of the valley	Peppermint	Emerald
Pink	Lily of the valley	Peppermint	Emerald
Pink	Lily of the valley	Peppermint	Emerald
Pink	Lily of the valley	Peppermint	Emerald
Pink	Lily of the valley	Peppermint	Emerald
Pink	Lily of the valley	Peppermint	Emerald
Pink	Lily of the valley	Peppermint	Emerald
Pink	Lily of the valley	Peppermint	Emerald
Pink	Lily of the valley	Peppermint	Emerald
Pink	Lily of the Valley	Peppermint	Emerald

	DAY	WESTERN ZODIAC	NATIVE AMERICAN BIRTH TIME ANIMAL	NATIVE AMERICAN SEASONAL ELEMENT
MAY	14	Taurus	N: Beaver S: Snake	N: Fire S: Earth
	15	Taurus	N: Beaver S: Snake	N: Fire S: Earth
	16	Taurus	N: Beaver S: Snake	N: Fire S: Earth
	17	Taurus	N: Beaver S: Snake	N: Fire S: Earth
	18	Taurus	N: Beaver S: Snake	N: Fire S: Earth
	19	Taurus	N: Beaver S: Snake	N: Fire S: Earth
	20	Taurus	N: Beaver S: Snake	N: Fire S: Earth
	21	Gemini	N: Deer S: Owl	N: Fire S: Earth
	22	Gemini	N: Deer S: Owl	N: Fire S: Earth
	23	Gemini	N: Deer S: Owl	N: Fire S: Earth
	24	Gemini	N: Deer S: Owl	N: Fire S: Earth
	25	Gemini	N: Deer S: Owl	N: Fire S: Earth
	26	Gemini	N: Deer S: Owl	N: Fire S: Earth
	27	Gemini	N: Deer S: Owl	N: Fire S: Earth
	28	Gemini	N: Deer S: Owl	N: Fire S: Earth
	29	Gemini	N: Deer S: Owl	N: Fire S: Earth
	30	Gemini	N: Deer S: Owl	N: Fire S: Earth
	31	Gemini	N: Deer S: Owl	N: Fire S: Earth
JUNE	1	Gemini	N: Deer S: Owl	N: Fire S: Earth
	2	Gemini	N: Deer S: Owl	N: Fire S: Earth
	3	Gemini	N: Deer S: Owl	N: Fire S: Earth
	4	Gemini	N: Deer S: Owl	N: Fire S: Earth
	5	Gemini	N: Deer S: Owl	N: Fire S: Earth
	6	Gemini	N: Deer S: Owl	N: Fire S: Earth
	7	Gemini	N: Deer S: Owl	N: Fire S: Earth
	8	Gemini	N: Deer S: Owl	N: Fire S: Earth
	9	Gemini	N: Deer S: Owl	N: Fire S: Earth
	10	Gemini	N: Deer S: Owl	N: Fire S: Earth
	11	Gemini	N: Deer S: Owl	N: Fire S: Earth
	12	Gemini	N: Deer S: Owl	N: Fire S: Earth
	13	Gemini	N: Deer S: Owl	N: Fire S: Earth
	14	Gemini	N: Deer S: Owl	N: Fire S: Earth
	15	Gemini	N: Deer S: Owl	N: Fire S: Earth
	16	Gemini	N: Deer S: Owl	N: Fire S: Earth
	17	Gemini	N: Deer S: Owl	N: Fire S: Earth
	18	Gemini	N: Deer S: Owl	N: Fire S: Earth
	19	Gemini	N: Deer S: Owl	N: Fire S: Earth
	20	Gemini	N: Deer S: Owl	N: Fire S: Earth
	21	Gemini	N: Woodpecker S: Snow goose	N: Water S: Air
	22	Cancer	N: Woodpecker S: Snow goose	N: Water S: Air
	23	Cancer	N: Woodpecker S: Snow goose	N: Water S: Air
	24	Cancer	N: Woodpecker S: Snow goose	N: Water S: Air
	25	Cancer	N: Woodpecker S: Snow goose	N: Water S: Air
	26	Cancer	N: Woodpecker S: Snow goose	N: Water S: Air
	27	Cancer	N: Woodpecker S: Snow goose	N: Water S: Air
	28	Cancer	N: Woodpecker S: Snow goose	N: Water S: Air
	29	Cancer	N: Woodpecker S: Snow goose	N: Water S: Air
	30	Cancer	N: Woodpecker S: Snow goose	N: Water S: Air

COLOR	FLOWERS	HERBS	GEMSTONES
Pink	Lily of the valley	Peppermint	Emerald
Pink	Lily of the valley	Peppermint	Emerald
Pink	Lily of the valley	Peppermint	Emerald
Pink	Lily of the valley	Peppermint	Emerald
Pink	Lily of the valley	Peppermint	Emerald
Pink	Lily of the valley	Peppermint	Emerald
Pink	Lily of the valley	Peppermint	Emerald
Yellow	Lily of the valley	Dill	Moonstone
Yellow	Lily of the valley	Dill	Moonstone
Yellow	Lily of the valley	Dill	Moonstone
Yellow	Lily of the valley	Dill	Moonstone
Yellow	Lily of the valley	Dill	Moonstone
Yellow	Lily of the valley	Dill	Moonstone
Yellow	Lily of the valley	Dill	Moonstone
Yellow	Lily of the valley	Dill	Moonstone
Yellow	Lily of the valley	Dill	Moonstone
Yellow	Lily of the valley	Dill	Moonstone
Yellow	Lily of the valley	Dill	Moonstone
Yellow	Rose	Dill	Moonstone
Yellow	Rose	Dill	Moonstone
Yellow	Rose	Dill	Moonstone
Yellow	Rose	Dill	Moonstone
Yellow	Rose	Dill	Moonstone
Yellow	Rose	Dill	Moonstone
Yellow	Rose	Dill	Moonstone
Yellow	Rose	Dill	Moonstone
Yellow	Rose	Dill	Moonstone
Yellow	Rose	Dill	Moonstone
Yellow	Rose	Dill	Moonstone
Yellow	Rose	Dill	Moonstone
Yellow	Rose	Dill	Moonstone
Yellow	Rose	Dill	Moonstone
Yellow	Rose	Dill	Moonstone
Yellow	Rose	Dill	Moonstone
Yellow	Rose	Dill	Moonstone
Yellow	Rose	Dill	Moonstone
Yellow	Rose	Dill	Moonstone
Yellow	Rose	Dill	Moonstone
Violet	Rose	Chamomile	Carnelian
Violet	Rose	Chamomile	Carnelian
Violet	Rose	Chamomile	Carnelian
Violet	Rose	Chamomile	Carnelian
Violet	Rose	Chamomile	Carnelian
Violet	Rose	Chamomile	Carnelian
Violet	Rose	Chamomile	Carnelian
Violet	Rose	Chamomile	Carnelian
Violet	Rose	Chamomile	Carnelian

▶

	DAY	WESTERN ZODIAC	NATIVE AMERICAN BIRTH TIME ANIMAL	NATIVE AMERICAN SEASONAL ELEMENT
JULY	1	Cancer	N: Woodpecker S: Snow goose	N: Water S: Air
	2	Cancer	N: Woodpecker S: Snow goose	N: Water S: Air
	3	Cancer	N: Woodpecker S: Snow goose	N: Water S: Air
	4	Cancer	N: Woodpecker S: Snow goose	N: Water S: Air
	5	Cancer	N: Woodpecker S: Snow goose	N: Water S: Air
	6	Cancer	N: Woodpecker S: Snow goose	N: Water S: Air
	7	Cancer	N: Woodpecker S: Snow goose	N: Water S: Air
	8	Cancer	N: Woodpecker S: Snow goose	N: Water S: Air
	9	Cancer	N: Woodpecker S: Snow goose	N: Water S: Air
	10	Cancer	N: Woodpecker S: Snow goose	N: Water S: Air
	11	Cancer	N: Woodpecker S: Snow goose	N: Water S: Air
	12	Cancer	N: Woodpecker S: Snow goose	N: Water S: Air
	13	Cancer	N: Woodpecker S: Snow goose	N: Water S: Air
	14	Cancer	N: Woodpecker S: Snow goose	N: Water S: Air
	15	Cancer	N: Woodpecker S: Snow goose	N: Water S: Air
	16	Cancer	N: Woodpecker S: Snow goose	N: Water S: Air
	17	Cancer	N: Woodpecker S: Snow goose	N: Water S: Air
	18	Cancer	N: Woodpecker S: Snow goose	N: Water S: Air
	19	Cancer	N: Woodpecker S: Snow goose	N: Water S: Air
	20	Cancer	N: Woodpecker S: Snow goose	N: Water S: Air
	21	Cancer	N: Woodpecker S: Snow goose	N: Water S: Air
	22	Cancer	N: Woodpecker S: Snow goose	N: Water S: Air
	23	Leo	N: Salmon S: Otter	N: Water S: Air
	24	Leo	N: Salmon S: Otter	N: Water S: Air
	25	Leo	N: Salmon S: Otter	N: Water S: Air
	26	Leo	N: Salmon S: Otter	N: Water S: Air
	27	Leo	N: Salmon S: Otter	N: Water S: Air
	28	Leo	N: Salmon S: Otter	N: Water S: Air
	29	Leo	N: Salmon S: Otter	N: Water S: Air
	30	Leo	N: Salmon S: Otter	N: Water S: Air
	31	Leo	N: Salmon S: Otter	N: Water S: Air
AUGUST	1	Leo	N: Salmon S: Otter	N: Water S: Air
	2	Leo	N: Salmon S: Otter	N: Water S: Air
	3	Leo	N: Salmon S: Otter	N: Water S: Air
	4	Leo	N: Salmon S: Otter	N: Water S: Air
	5	Leo	N: Salmon S: Otter	N: Water S: Air
	6	Leo	N: Salmon S: Otter	N: Water S: Air
	7	Leo	N: Salmon S: Otter	N: Water S: Air
	8	Leo	N: Salmon S: Otter	N: Water S: Air
	9	Leo	N: Salmon S: Otter	N: Water S: Air
	10	Leo	N: Salmon S: Otter	N: Water S: Air
	11	Leo	N: Salmon S: Otter	N: Water S: Air
	12	Leo	N: Salmon S: Otter	N: Water S: Air
	13	Leo	N: Salmon S: Otter	N: Water S: Air
	14	Leo	N: Salmon S: Otter	N: Water S: Air
	15	Leo	N: Salmon S: Otter	N: Water S: Air

COLOR	FLOWERS	HERBS	GEMSTONES
Violet	Delphinium	Chamomile	Carnelian
Violet	Delphinium	Chamomile	Carnelian
Violet	Delphinium	Chamomile	Carnelian
Violet	Delphinium	Chamomile	Carnelian
Violet	Delphinium	Chamomile	Carnelian
Violet	Delphinium	Chamomile	Carnelian
Violet	Delphinium	Chamomile	Carnelian
Violet	Delphinium	Chamomile	Carnelian
Violet	Delphinium	Chamomile	Carnelian
Violet	Delphinium	Chamomile	Carnelian
Violet	Delphinium	Chamomile	Carnelian
Violet	Delphinium	Chamomile	Carnelian
Violet	Delphinium	Chamomile	Carnelian
Violet	Delphinium	Chamomile	Carnelian
Violet	Delphinium	Chamomile	Carnelian
Violet	Delphinium	Chamomile	Carnelian
Violet	Delphinium	Chamomile	Carnelian
Violet	Delphinium	Chamomile	Carnelian
Violet	Delphinium	Chamomile	Carnelian
Violet	Delphinium	Chamomile	Carnelian
Violet	Delphinium	Chamomile	Carnelian
Violet	Delphinium	Chamomile	Carnelian
Orange	Delphinium	Saffron	Sardonyx
Orange	Delphinium	Saffron	Sardonyx
Orange	Delphinium	Saffron	Sardonyx
Orange	Delphinium	Saffron	Sardonyx
Orange	Delphinium	Saffron	Sardonyx
Orange	Delphinium	Saffron	Sardonyx
Orange	Delphinium	Saffron	Sardonyx
Orange	Delphinium	Saffron	Sardonyx
Orange	Delphinium	Saffron	Sardonyx
Orange	Poppy	Saffron	Sardonyx
Orange	Poppy	Saffron	Sardonyx
Orange	Poppy	Saffron	Sardonyx
Orange	Poppy	Saffron	Sardonyx
Orange	Poppy	Saffron	Sardonyx
Orange	Poppy	Saffron	Sardonyx
Orange	Poppy	Saffron	Sardonyx
Orange	Poppy	Saffron	Sardonyx
Orange	Poppy	Saffron	Sardonyx
Orange	Poppy	Saffron	Sardonyx
Orange	Poppy	Saffron	Sardonyx
Orange	Poppy	Saffron	Sardonyx
Orange	Poppy	Saffron	Sardonyx
Orange	Poppy	Saffron	Sardonyx
Orange	Poppy	Saffron	Sardonyx

	DAY	WESTERN ZODIAC	NATIVE AMERICAN BIRTH TIME ANIMAL	NATIVE AMERICAN SEASONAL ELEMENT
AUGUST	16	Leo	N: Salmon S: Otter	N: Water S: Air
	17	Leo	N: Salmon S: Otter	N: Water S: Air
	18	Leo	N: Salmon S: Otter	N: Water S: Air
	19	Leo	N: Salmon S: Otter	N: Water S: Air
	20	Leo	N: Salmon S: Otter	N: Water S: Air
	21	Leo	N: Salmon S: Otter	N: Water S: Air
	22	Leo	N: Salmon S: Otter	N: Water S: Air
	23	Virgo	N: Brown bear S: Wolf	N: Water S: Air
	24	Virgo	N: Brown bear S: Wolf	N: Water S: Air
	25	Virgo	N: Brown bear S: Wolf	N: Water S: Air
	26	Virgo	N: Brown bear S: Wolf	N: Water S: Air
	27	Virgo	N: Brown bear S: Wolf	N: Water S: Air
	28	Virgo	N: Brown bear S: Wolf	N: Water S: Air
	29	Virgo	N: Brown bear S: Wolf	N: Water S: Air
	30	Virgo	N: Brown bear S: Wolf	N: Water S: Air
	31	Virgo	N: Brown bear S: Wolf	N: Water S: Air
SEPTEMBER	1	Virgo	N: Brown bear S: Wolf	N: Water S: Air
	2	Virgo	N: Brown bear S: Wolf	N: Water S: Air
	3	Virgo	N: Brown bear S: Wolf	N: Water S: Air
	4	Virgo	N: Brown bear S: Wolf	N: Water S: Air
	5	Virgo	N: Brown bear S: Wolf	N: Water S: Air
	6	Virgo	N: Brown bear S: Wolf	N: Water S: Air
	7	Virgo	N: Brown bear S: Wolf	N: Water S: Air
	8	Virgo	N: Brown bear S: Wolf	N: Water S: Air
	9	Virgo	N: Brown bear S: Wolf	N: Water S: Air
	10	Virgo	N: Brown bear S: Wolf	N: Water S: Air
	11	Virgo	N: Brown bear S: Wolf	N: Water S: Air
	12	Virgo	N: Brown bear S: Wolf	N: Water S: Air
	13	Virgo	N: Brown bear S: Wolf	N: Water S: Air
	14	Virgo	N: Brown bear S: Wolf	N: Water S: Air
	15	Virgo	N: Brown bear S: Wolf	N: Water S: Air
	16	Virgo	N: Brown bear S: Wolf	N: Water S: Air
	17	Virgo	N: Brown bear S: Wolf	N: Water S: Air
	18	Virgo	N: Brown bear S: Wolf	N: Water S: Air
	19	Virgo	N: Brown bear S: Wolf	N: Water S: Air
	20	Virgo	N: Brown bear S: Wolf	N: Water S: Air
	21	Virgo	N: Brown bear S: Wolf	N: Water S: Air
	22	Virgo	N: Brown bear S: Wolf	N: Water S: Air
	23	Libra	N: Raven S: Hawk	N: Earth S: Fire
	24	Libra	N: Raven S: Hawk	N: Earth S: Fire
	25	Libra	N: Raven S: Hawk	N: Earth S: Fire
	26	Libra	N: Raven S: Hawk	N: Earth S: Fire
	27	Libra	N: Raven S: Hawk	N: Earth S: Fire
	28	Libra	N: Raven S: Hawk	N: Earth S: Fire
	29	Libra	N: Raven S: Hawk	N: Earth S: Fire
	30	Libra	N: Raven S: Hawk	N: Earth S: Fire

COLOR	FLOWERS	HERBS	GEMSTONES
Orange	Poppy	Saffron	Sardonyx
Orange	Poppy	Saffron	Sardonyx
Orange	Poppy	Saffron	Sardonyx
Orange	Poppy	Saffron	Sardonyx
Orange	Poppy	Saffron	Sardonyx
Orange	Poppy	Saffron	Sardonyx
Orange	Poppy	Saffron	Sardonyx
Brown	Poppy	Valerian	Sapphire
Brown	Poppy	Valerian	Sapphire
Brown	Poppy	Valerian	Sapphire
Brown	Poppy	Valerian	Sapphire
Brown	Poppy	Valerian	Sapphire
Brown	Poppy	Valerian	Sapphire
Brown	Poppy	Valerian	Sapphire
Brown	Poppy	Valerian	Sapphire
Brown	Poppy	Valerian	Sapphire
Brown	Aster	Valerian	Sapphire
Brown	Aster	Valerian	Sapphire
Brown	Aster	Valerian	Sapphire
Brown	Aster	Valerian	Sapphire
Brown	Aster	Valerian	Sapphire
Brown	Aster	Valerian	Sapphire
Brown	Aster	Valerian	Sapphire
Brown	Aster	Valerian	Sapphire
Brown	Aster	Valerian	Sapphire
Brown	Aster	Valerian	Sapphire
Brown	Aster	Valerian	Sapphire
Brown	Aster	Valerian	Sapphire
Brown	Aster	Valerian	Sapphire
Brown	Aster	Valerian	Sapphire
Brown	Aster	Valerian	Sapphire
Brown	Aster	Valerian	Sapphire
Brown	Aster	Valerian	Sapphire
Brown	Aster	Valerian	Sapphire
Brown	Aster	Valerian	Sapphire
Brown	Aster	Valerian	Sapphire
Brown	Aster	Valerian	Sapphire
Indigo	Aster	Dandelion	Opal
Indigo	Aster	Dandelion	Opal
Indigo	Aster	Dandelion	Opal
Indigo	Aster	Dandelion	Opal
Indigo	Aster	Dandelion	Opal
Indigo	Aster	Dandelion	Opal
Indigo	Aster	Dandelion	Opal
Indigo	Aster	Dandelion	Opal

	DAY	WESTERN ZODIAC	NATIVE AMERICAN BIRTH TIME ANIMAL	NATIVE AMERICAN SEASONAL ELEMENT
OCTOBER	1	Libra	N: Raven S: Hawk	N: Earth S: Fire
	2	Libra	N: Raven S: Hawk	N: Earth S: Fire
	3	Libra	N: Raven S: Hawk	N: Earth S: Fire
	4	Libra	N: Raven S: Hawk	N: Earth S: Fire
	5	Libra	N: Raven S: Hawk	N: Earth S: Fire
	6	Libra	N: Raven S: Hawk	N: Earth S: Fire
	7	Libra	N: Raven S: Hawk	N: Earth S: Fire
	8	Libra	N: Raven S: Hawk	N: Earth S: Fire
	9	Libra	N: Raven S: Hawk	N: Earth S: Fire
	10	Libra	N: Raven S: Hawk	N: Earth S: Fire
	11	Libra	N: Raven S: Hawk	N: Earth S: Fire
	12	Libra	N: Raven S: Hawk	N: Earth S: Fire
	13	Libra	N: Raven S: Hawk	N: Earth S: Fire
	14	Libra	N: Raven S: Hawk	N: Earth S: Fire
	15	Libra	N: Raven S: Hawk	N: Earth S: Fire
	16	Libra	N: Raven S: Hawk	N: Earth S: Fire
	17	Libra	N: Raven S: Hawk	N: Earth S: Fire
	18	Libra	N: Raven S: Hawk	N: Earth S: Fire
	19	Libra	N: Raven S: Hawk	N: Earth S: Fire
	20	Libra	N: Raven S: Hawk	N: Earth S: Fire
	21	Libra	N: Raven S: Hawk	N: Earth S: Fire
	22	Libra	N: Raven S: Hawk	N: Earth S: Fire
	23	Scorpio	N: Snake S: Beaver	N: Earth S: Fire
	24	Scorpio	N: Snake S: Beaver	N: Earth S: Fire
	25	Scorpio	N: Snake S: Beaver	N: Earth S: Fire
	26	Scorpio	N: Snake S: Beaver	N: Earth S: Fire
	27	Scorpio	N: Snake S: Beaver	N: Earth S: Fire
	28	Scorpio	N: Snake S: Beaver	N: Earth S: Fire
	29	Scorpio	N: Snake S: Beaver	N: Earth S: Fire
	30	Scorpio	N: Snake S: Beaver	N: Earth S: Fire
	31	Scorpio	N: Snake S: Beaver	N: Earth S: Fire
NOVEMBER	1	Scorpio	N: Snake S: Beaver	N: Earth S: Fire
	2	Scorpio	N: Snake S: Beaver	N: Earth S: Fire
	3	Scorpio	N: Snake S: Beaver	N: Earth S: Fire
	4	Scorpio	N: Snake S: Beaver	N: Earth S: Fire
	5	Scorpio	N: Snake S: Beaver	N: Earth S: Fire
	6	Scorpio	N: Snake S: Beaver	N: Earth S: Fire
	7	Scorpio	N: Snake S: Beaver	N: Earth S: Fire
	8	Scorpio	N: Snake S: Beaver	N: Earth S: Fire
	9	Scorpio	N: Snake S: Beaver	N: Earth S: Fire
	10	Scorpio	N: Snake S: Beaver	N: Earth S: Fire
	11	Scorpio	N: Snake S: Beaver	N: Earth S: Fire
	12	Scorpio	N: Snake S: Beaver	N: Earth S: Fire
	13	Scorpio	N: Snake S: Beaver	N: Earth S: Fire
	14	Scorpio	N: Snake S: Beaver	N: Earth S: Fire
	15	Scorpio	N: Snake S: Beaver	N: Earth S: Fire

COLOR	FLOWERS	HERBS	GEMSTONES
Indigo	Marigold	Dandelion	Opal
Indigo	Marigold	Dandelion	Opal
Indigo	Marigold	Dandelion	Opal
Indigo	Marigold	Dandelion	Opal
Indigo	Marigold	Dandelion	Opal
Indigo	Marigold	Dandelion	Opal
Indigo	Marigold	Dandelion	Opal
Indigo	Marigold	Dandelion	Opal
Indigo	Marigold	Dandelion	Opal
Indigo	Marigold	Dandelion	Opal
Indigo	Marigold	Dandelion	Opal
Indigo	Marigold	Dandelion	Opal
Indigo	Marigold	Dandelion	Opal
Indigo	Marigold	Dandelion	Opal
Indigo	Marigold	Dandelion	Opal
Indigo	Marigold	Dandelion	Opal
Indigo	Marigold	Dandelion	Opal
Indigo	Marigold	Dandelion	Opal
Indigo	Marigold	Dandelion	Opal
Indigo	Marigold	Dandelion	Opal
Indigo	Marigold	Dandelion	Opal
Indigo	Marigold	Dandelion	Opal
Black	Marigold	Basil	Topaz
Black	Marigold	Basil	Topaz
Black	Marigold	Basil	Topaz
Black	Marigold	Basil	Topaz
Black	Marigold	Basil	Topaz
Black	Marigold	Basil	Topaz
Black	Marigold	Basil	Topaz
Black	Marigold	Basil	Topaz
Black	Marigold	Basil	Topaz
Black	Chrysanthemum	Basil	Topaz
Black	Chrysanthemum	Basil	Topaz
Black	Chrysanthemum	Basil	Topaz
Black	Chrysanthemum	Basil	Topaz
Black	Chrysanthemum	Basil	Topaz
Black	Chrysanthemum	Basil	Topaz
Black	Chrysanthemum	Basil	Topaz
Black	Chrysanthemum	Basil	Topaz
Black	Chrysanthemum	Basil	Topaz
Black	Chrysanthemum	Basil	Topaz
Black	Chrysanthemum	Basil	Topaz
Black	Chrysanthemum	Basil	Topaz
Black	Chrysanthemum	Basil	Topaz
Black	Chrysanthemum	Basil	Topaz
Black	Chrysanthemum	Basil	Topaz

	DAY	WESTERN ZODIAC	NATIVE AMERICAN BIRTH TIME ANIMAL	NATIVE AMERICAN SEASONAL ELEMENT
NOVEMBER	16	Scorpio	N: Snake S: Beaver	N: Earth S: Fire
	17	Scorpio	N: Snake S: Beaver	N: Earth S: Fire
	18	Scorpio	N: Snake S: Beaver	N: Earth S: Fire
	19	Scorpio	N: Snake S: Beaver	N: Earth S: Fire
	20	Scorpio	N: Snake S: Beaver	N: Earth S: Fire
	21	Scorpio	N: Snake S: Beaver	N: Earth S: Fire
	22	Sagittarius	N: Owl S: Deer	N: Earth S: Fire
	23	Sagittarius	N: Owl S: Deer	N: Earth S: Fire
	24	Sagittarius	N: Owl S: Deer	N: Earth S: Fire
	25	Sagittarius	N: Owl S: Deer	N: Earth S: Fire
	26	Sagittarius	N: Owl S: Deer	N: Earth S: Fire
	27	Sagittarius	N: Owl S: Deer	N: Earth S: Fire
	28	Sagittarius	N: Owl S: Deer	N: Earth S: Fire
	29	Sagittarius	N: Owl S: Deer	N: Earth S: Fire
	30	Sagittarius	N: Owl S: Deer	N: Earth S: Fire
DECEMBER	1	Sagittarius	N: Owl S: Deer	N: Earth S: Fire
	2	Sagittarius	N: Owl S: Deer	N: Earth S: Fire
	3	Sagittarius	N: Owl S: Deer	N: Earth S: Fire
	4	Sagittarius	N: Owl S: Deer	N: Earth S: Fire
	5	Sagittarius	N: Owl S: Deer	N: Earth S: Fire
	6	Sagittarius	N: Owl S: Deer	N: Earth S: Fire
	7	Sagittarius	N: Owl S: Deer	N: Earth S: Fire
	8	Sagittarius	N: Owl S: Deer	N: Earth S: Fire
	9	Sagittarius	N: Owl S: Deer	N: Earth S: Fire
	10	Sagittarius	N: Owl S: Deer	N: Earth S: Fire
	11	Sagittarius	N: Owl S: Deer	N: Earth S: Fire
	12	Sagittarius	N: Owl S: Deer	N: Earth S: Fire
	13	Sagittarius	N: Owl S: Deer	N: Earth S: Fire
	14	Sagittarius	N: Owl S: Deer	N: Earth S: Fire
	15	Sagittarius	N: Owl S: Deer	N: Earth S: Fire
	16	Sagittarius	N: Owl S: Deer	N: Earth S: Fire
	17	Sagittarius	N: Owl S: Deer	N: Earth S: Fire
	18	Sagittarius	N: Owl S: Deer	N: Earth S: Fire
	19	Sagittarius	N: Owl S: Deer	N: Earth S: Fire
	20	Sagittarius	N: Owl S: Deer	N: Earth S: Fire
	21	Sagittarius	N: Owl S: Deer	N: Earth S: Fire
	22	Capricorn	N: Snow goose S: Woodpecker	N: Air S: Water
	23	Capricorn	N: Snow goose S: Woodpecker	N: Air S: Water
	24	Capricorn	N: Snow goose S: Woodpecker	N: Air S: Water
	25	Capricorn	N: Snow goose S: Woodpecker	N: Air S: Water
	26	Capricorn	N: Snow goose S: Woodpecker	N: Air S: Water
	27	Capricorn	N: Snow goose S: Woodpecker	N: Air S: Water
	28	Capricorn	N: Snow goose S: Woodpecker	N: Air S: Water
	29	Capricorn	N: Snow goose S: Woodpecker	N: Air S: Water
	30	Capricorn	N: Snow goose S: Woodpecker	N: Air S: Water
	31	Capricorn	N: Snow goose S: Woodpecker	N: Air S: Water

COLOR	FLOWERS	HERBS	GEMSTONES
Black	Chrysanthemum	Basil	Topaz
Black	Chrysanthemum	Basil	Topaz
Black	Chrysanthemum	Basil	Topaz
Black	Chrysanthemum	Basil	Topaz
Black	Chrysanthemum	Basil	Topaz
Black	Chrysanthemum	Basil	Topaz
Light blue	Chrysanthemum	Sage	Turquoise
Light blue	Chrysanthemum	Sage	Turquoise
Light blue	Chrysanthemum	Sage	Turquoise
Light blue	Chrysanthemum	Sage	Turquoise
Light blue	Chrysanthemum	Sage	Turquoise
Light blue	Chrysanthemum	Sage	Turquoise
Light blue	Chrysanthemum	Sage	Turquoise
Light blue	Chrysanthemum	Sage	Turquoise
Light blue	Chrysanthemum	Sage	Turquoise
Light blue	Holly	Sage	Turquoise
Light blue	Holly	Sage	Turquoise
Light blue	Holly	Sage	Turquoise
Light blue	Holly	Sage	Turquoise
Light blue	Holly	Sage	Turquoise
Light blue	Holly	Sage	Turquoise
Light blue	Holly	Sage	Turquoise
Light blue	Holly	Sage	Turquoise
Light blue	Holly	Sage	Turquoise
Light blue	Holly	Sage	Turquoise
Light blue	Holly	Sage	Turquoise
Light blue	Holly	Sage	Turquoise
Light blue	Holly	Sage	Turquoise
Light blue	Holly	Sage	Turquoise
Light blue	Holly	Sage	Turquoise
Light blue	Holly	Sage	Turquoise
Light blue	Holly	Sage	Turquoise
Light blue	Holly	Sage	Turquoise
Light blue	Holly	Sage	Turquoise
Green	Holly	Comfrey	Garnet
Green	Holly	Comfrey	Garnet
Green	Holly	Comfrey	Garnet
Green	Holly	Comfrey	Garnet
Green	Holly	Comfrey	Garnet
Green	Holly	Comfrey	Garnet
Green	Holly	Comfrey	Garnet
Green	Holly	Comfrey	Garnet
Green	Holly	Comfrey	Garnet
Green	Holly	Comfrey	Garnet
Green	Holly	Comfrey	Garnet

Your birthday by the month

In Chinese astrology, the hour, month, and year of your birth help to define your personality. The year of your birth is your dominant sign in Chinese astrology and provides information about your underlying personality (see pages 31–33). Your secret or hidden self is determined by the hour in which you were born (see pages 10–11). The month of your birth provides insight into your love life. The animal sign ruling over this month reveals your character in intimate relationships. See the table below for insights into your love life.

MONTH OF BIRTH = LOVE

YOUR LOVE LIFE

MONTH	ANIMAL	LOVE ATTRIBUTES
December	Rat Animal motto: "I think."	Rats are innovative when it comes to wooing their chosen mates. They attend to the little details of romance and seduction and take great pride in their personal appearance. Rats are usually attracted to committed, long-term relationships that provide them with plenty of emotional support.
January	Ox Animal motto: "I am patient."	The Ox is not a passionate or romantic sign, as oxen focus more on work than on love. However, they do have an eye for beauty and can be sensuous when moved. They have a great deal of sexual stamina but are not overly demonstrative in public. They will show how much they care by staying monogamous and providing security for their partners.
February	Tiger Animal motto: "I have courage."	Tigers are full of zest and personal charisma, romping from one romance to another. Ruled by their hearts, they follow their instincts when it comes to romance—they will rarely employ logic or reflect on the new object of their affection.
March	Rabbit Animal motto: "I am discreet."	Rabbits are renowned for their sensual orientation. They are sensitive, irresistible, indulgent, and romantic, investing much time in their intimate relationships. Rabbits are attracted to confident and successful partners.

April	Dragon Animal motto: "I am majestic."	Dragons are magnificent lovers due to their high energy and vibrant personalities. They feel a need to be loved and wish for the adoration of others. Loving the new and the exciting, Dragons tend to be in love with love, leaving commitment for later in their lives.
May	Snake Animal motto: "I have sense."	Snakes are renowned for their hypnotic beauty and seductive streak and are able to mesmerize everyone around them. Although cool and distant, snakes can display hidden depths when they have committed themselves to a partner.
June	Horse Animal motto: "I run free."	Horses are virile and physically exhausting as lovers. Blessed with youthful vitality and enthusiasm, Horses leap into love affairs with wild abandon. They are forever restless, wanting change and variety and tending toward promiscuous lifestyles.
July	Sheep Animal motto: "I adapt."	Sheep are sensuous, with very active sex drives. Compassionate and understanding, Sheep are romantic and intuitive, giving and expecting generosity and attention.
August	Monkey Animal motto: "I entertain."	Monkeys are fun and lively lovers who are not overly concerned about their morals in the bedroom. As they love a challenge, Monkeys are not above competing for the affections of those they desire.
September	Rooster Animal motto: "I am resilient."	Roosters like to be in control of their love life and value anyone who showers them with praise. They are renowned for their skill and stamina in the bedroom. Roosters are very keen to win the approval of their loved ones and do so with lavish gifts, outings, and holidays.
October	Dog Animal motto: "I am loyal."	Dogs are dedicated and loyal lovers. They do not take affairs of the heart lightly and will take some time to consider whether their attraction for someone is worth it in the long term. Dogs are easily hurt and disappointed. However, once they are in a committed relationship, they can be affectionate, protective, and self-sacrificing.
November	Pig Animal motto: "I am eager."	Pigs are sensual beings who know how to engage all the senses in wild abandon, with no care for the consequences. Pigs' lovemaking is enduring, tender and compassionate. They are openly demonstrative with their partners and give them a lot of freedom.

Your birthday by the year

Each of the twelve animals of Chinese astrology has distinct personality traits associated with it. In every twelve-year cycle, one of these animals governs each year. Using the Chinese Year Chart on pages 31–33, look under the year you were born for your associated animal and its element.

The animal that corresponds to your year of birth is your dominant sign. It is believed that you share the personality traits of your dominant sign. These are the traits that others see—the ones you show to the world. However, they can be moderated by the traits of the animals ruling over your month (see pages 28–29) and time of birth (see pages 10–11). Combining these three aspects will result in a detailed, unique character profile for each person (see pages 40–45).

ORIGIN OF THE TWELVE-YEAR ANIMAL CYCLE

The great Buddha is said to have lived around the years 563 to 483 BC. This was a time when myths, legends, and tradition were considered important aspects of daily life.

Legend says that when the great Buddha found enlightenment and was ready to leave the earth, he invited all the land's creatures to his kingdom to say farewell before his departure. Only twelve animals arrived, in this order: The rat, the ox, the tiger, the rabbit, the dragon, the snake, the horse, the sheep, the monkey, the rooster, the dog, and, finally, the pig. To thank the animals for answering his call, Buddha decided to celebrate each of them. Their reward was that each new year would be celebrated in their honor. Accordingly, in every twelve-year cycle, each of the twelve animals is celebrated in turn. This means that people born during a specific year will be influenced, in terms of personality and life events, by the animal the year celebrates.

The Chinese Lunar Calendar

Unlike the Western system, which records time in solar years (a solar year is Earth's 365-day rotation around the sun), the Chinese system measures time in lunar years, which follow the moon's orbit around Earth. The Chinese New Year falls on a different date every year, either in January or in February. If you were born during these months, consult the Chinese Year Chart (see below and the following pages) to find out which animal and element dominate the year you were born.

KEY PERSONALITY CHARACTERISTICS	
ANIMAL	KEY CHARACTERISTICS
Rat	Ambitious, intelligent
Ox	Tenacious, patient
Tiger	Courageous, dominant
Rabbit	Flexible, balanced
Dragon	Powerful, dynamic
Snake	Wise, influential
Horse	Full of vitality, agile
Sheep	Serene, peaceful
Monkey	Witty, clever
Rooster	Alert, honorable
Dog	Judicious, loyal
Pig	Carefree, contented

CHINESE YEAR CHART 1900–2019
NOTE: DATES VARY ACCORDING TO DIFFERENT AUTHORITIES

LUNAR YEAR	DATE FROM	DATE TO	DOMINANT ANIMAL	DOMINANT ELEMENT
1900	3/31/00	2/18/01	Rat	Metal
1901	2/19/01	2/7/02	Ox	Metal
1902	2/8/02	1/28/03	Tiger	Water
1903	1/29/03	2/15/04	Rabbit	Water
1904	2/16/04	2/3/05	Dragon	Wood
1905	2/4/05	1/24/06	Snake	Wood
1906	1/25/06	2/12/07	Horse	Fire
1907	2/13/07	2/1/08	Sheep	Fire
1908	2/2/08	1/21/09	Monkey	Earth
1909	1/22/09	2/9/10	Rooster	Earth
1910	2/10/10	1/29/11	Dog	Metal
1911	1/30/11	2/17/12	Pig	Metal
1912	2/18/12	2/5/13	Rat	Water
1913	2/6/13	1/25/14	Ox	Water
1914	1/26/14	2/13/15	Tiger	Wood
1915	2/14/15	2/2/16	Rabbit	Wood

▶

LUNAR YEAR	DATE FROM	DATE TO	DOMINANT ANIMAL	DOMINANT ELEMENT
1916	2/3/16	1/22/17	Dragon	Fire
1917	1/23/17	2/10/18	Snake	Fire
1918	2/11/18	1/31/19	Horse	Earth
1919	2/1/19	2/19/20	Sheep	Earth
1920	2/20/20	2/7/21	Monkey	Metal
1921	2/8/21	1/27/22	Rooster	Metal
1922	1/28/22	2/15/23	Dog	Water
1923	2/16/23	2/4/24	Pig	Water
1924	2/5/24	1/24/25	Rat	Wood
1925	1/25/25	2/12/26	Ox	Wood
1926	2/13/26	2/1/27	Tiger	Fire
1927	2/2/27	1/22/28	Rabbit	Fire
1928	1/23/28	2/9/29	Dragon	Earth
1929	2/10/29	1/29/30	Snake	Earth
1930	1/30/30	2/16/31	Horse	Metal
1931	2/17/31	2/5/32	Sheep	Metal
1932	2/6/32	1/25/33	Monkey	Water
1933	1/26/33	2/13/34	Rooster	Water
1934	2/14/34	2/3/35	Dog	Wood
1935	2/4/35	1/23/36	Pig	Wood
1936	1/24/36	2/10/37	Rat	Fire
1937	2/11/37	1/30/38	Ox	Fire
1938	1/31/38	2/18/39	Tiger	Earth
1939	2/19/39	2/7/40	Rabbit	Earth
1940	2/8/40	1/26/41	Dragon	Metal
1941	1/27/41	2/14/42	Snake	Metal
1942	2/15/42	2/4/43	Horse	Water
1943	2/5/43	1/24/44	Sheep	Water
1944	1/25/44	2/12/45	Monkey	Wood
1945	2/13/45	2/1/46	Rooster	Wood
1946	2/2/46	1/21/47	Dog	Fire
1947	1/22/47	2/9/48	Pig	Fire
1948	2/10/48	1/28/49	Rat	Earth
1949	1/29/49	2/16/50	Ox	Earth
1950	2/17/50	2/5/51	Tiger	Metal
1951	2/6/51	1/26/52	Rabbit	Metal
1952	1/27/52	2/13/53	Dragon	Water
1953	2/14/53	2/2/54	Snake	Water
1954	2/3/54	1/23/55	Horse	Wood
1955	1/24/55	2/11/56	Sheep	Wood
1956	2/12/56	1/30/57	Monkey	Fire
1957	1/31/57	2/17/58	Rooster	Fire
1958	2/18/58	2/7/59	Dog	Earth
1959	2/8/59	1/27/60	Pig	Earth
1960	1/28/60	2/14/61	Rat	Metal
1961	2/15/61	2/4/62	Ox	Metal
1962	2/5/62	1/24/63	Tiger	Water
1963	1/25/63	2/12/64	Rabbit	Water
1964	2/13/64	2/1/65	Dragon	Wood
1965	2/2/65	1/20/66	Snake	Wood
1966	1/21/66	2/8/67	Horse	Fire
1967	2/9/67	1/29/68	Sheep	Fire

LUNAR YEAR	DATE FROM	DATE TO	DOMINANT ANIMAL	DOMINANT ELEMENT
1968	1/30/68	2/16/69	Monkey	Earth
1969	2/17/69	2/5/70	Rooster	Earth
1970	2/6/70	1/26/71	Dog	Metal
1971	1/27/71	21/15/72	Pig	Metal
1972	1/16/72	2/2/73	Rat	Water
1973	2/3/73	1/22/74	Ox	Water
1974	1/23/74	2/10/75	Tiger	Wood
1975	2/11/75	1/30/76	Rabbit	Wood
1976	1/31/76	2/17/77	Dragon	Fire
1977	2/18/77	2/6/78	Snake	Fire
1978	2/7/78	1/27/79	Horse	Earth
1979	1/28/79	2/15/80	Sheep	Earth
1980	2/16/80	2/4/81	Monkey	Metal
1981	2/5/81	1/24/82	Rooster	Metal
1982	1/25/82	2/12/83	Dog	Water
1983	2/13/83	2/1/84	Pig	Water
1984	2/2/84	2/19/85	Rat	Wood
1985	2/20/85	2/8/86	Ox	Wood
1986	2/9/86	1/28/87	Tiger	Fire
1987	1/29/87	2/16/88	Rabbit	Fire
1988	2/17/88	2/5/89	Dragon	Earth
1989	2/6/89	1/26/90	Snake	Earth
1990	1/27/90	2/14/91	Horse	Metal
1991	2/15/91	2/3/92	Sheep	Metal
1992	2/4/92	1/22/93	Monkey	Water
1993	1/23/93	2/9/94	Rooster	Water
1994	2/10/94	1/30/95	Dog	Wood
1995	1/31/95	2/18/96	Pig	Wood
1996	2/19/96	2/6/97	Rat	Fire
1997	2/7/97	1/27/98	Ox	Fire
1998	1/28/98	2/15/99	Tiger	Earth
1999	2/16/99	2/4/2000	Rabbit	Earth
2000	2/5/2000	1/23/2001	Dragon	Metal
2001	1/24/01	2/11/2002	Snake	Metal
2002	2/12/02	1/31/2003	Horse	Water
2003	2/1/03	1/21/2004	Sheep	Water
2004	1/22/04	2/8/2005	Monkey	Wood
2005	2/9/05	1/28/2006	Rooster	Wood
2006	1/29/06	2/17/2007	Dog	Fire
2007	2/18/07	2/6/2008	Pig	Fire
2008	2/7/08	1/25/2009	Rat	Earth
2009	1/26/09	2/13/2010	Ox	Earth
2010	2/14/10	2/2/2011	Tiger	Metal
2011	2/3/11	1/22/2012	Rabbit	Metal
2012	1/23/12	2/9/2013	Dragon	Water
2013	2/10/13	1/30/2014	Snake	Water
2014	1/31/14	2/18/2015	Horse	Wood
2015	2/19/15	2/7/2016	Sheep	Wood
2016	2/8/16	1/27/2017	Monkey	Fire
2017	1/28/17	2/15/2018	Rooster	Fire
2018	2/16/18	2/4/2019	Dog	Earth
2019	2/5/19	1/24/2020	Pig	Earth

Your lucky birth number

For centuries, mystics and philosophers, mathematicians and alchemists have experimented with numerical systems to explore the significance of numbers in our lives. For instance, it was said that we should never state our age aloud—once in possession of the numbers, the ever-listening Forces of Darkness would have the power to cause great harm to the body or soul. How much of that old belief lingers today in people's reluctance to reveal their age?

Birth numbers or personal destiny numbers are easy to calculate. Discarding all zeros, total your date, month, and year of birth, and reduce that figure to one digit.

If you were born on June 27, 1960, number four would be your personal destiny number:

$$2 + 7 + 6 + 1 + 9 + 6 = 31 = 3 + 1 = 4$$

Each primary number or birth number from one to nine has a specific meaning and is governed by a planetary force.

If you were born on September 20, 1939, number thirty-three would be your personal destiny number:

$$2 + 9 + 1 + 9 + 3 + 9 = 33$$

This is a master number, along with eleven and twenty-two, which in many numerological systems do not get reduced further to a single digit. These numbers often belong to people whose destiny is

important and unusual. They have strong psychic ability and appear to be highly evolved spiritually. The positive and negative influences of numbers on our personal destinies are vast and well documented. To practice the art of numerology—predicting the future with numbers—you do not need a good knowledge of mathematics. While this method of fortunetelling is quite simple to practice, it is nonetheless an interesting and powerful way to discover important personal character traits, enabling you to understand yourself better.

WHAT YOUR BIRTH NUMBER MEANS

NUMBER	MEANING
1	Ruled by the sun, this number, truly indivisible, signifies power, independence, responsibility, and action. People with this birth number are leaders rather than followers and can be overbearing or intolerant.
2	This is the number ruled by the moon, the planet that fosters harmony on Earth by favoring love and union, diplomacy and tact, negotiation and settlement, and all cooperative ventures of genuine mutual benefit to the participants.
3	A lucky number, governed by the planet Jupiter, which enhances individual optimism, sociability, and creative self-expression. Conversely, three may indicate procrastination, carelessness, and extravagance.
4	This number is ruled by the planet Uranus, which brings efficiency and practicality to those born under its influence. The negative possibilities of this number include prejudice and resentment.
5	Five, a quixotic number of quicksilver temperament and ruled by the changeable planet Mercury, is usually the birth number of a communicator or someone extremely creative and possibly artistic.
6	Ruled by the planet Venus, this number promises fame and possibly the gift of prophecy to its sympathetic, loving children, who may suffer from anxiety or a jealous temper.
7	A very lucky number, under the influence of the planet Neptune. They possess fine powers of sympathy, intuition, and second sight but they may be prone to moodiness and depression.
8	Eight, ruled by the sometimes ruthless planetary energy of Saturn, is a symbol of survival. It indicates an analytical, efficient, and controlled personality that can sometimes be intolerant.
9	A multiple of lucky three, and hence also a lucky number, nine is ruled by Mars. This is the planet of compassion and generosity on the one hand, and self-centeredness and emotional volatility on the other.
11	This is a master number that resonates with the energy of the moon. Elevens are concerned with spiritual evolvement, which often leads to an unusual destiny. They must avoid vanity and the tendency to be opinionated.
22	This is a master number that resonates with the energy of Uranus. Twenty-twos have high ideals and goals and are extremely psychic. They may expect far too much from others and become tyrannical.
33	This is a master number that resonates with the energy of Venus. Thirty-threes are compassionate on a global scale, which can make them prone to oversensitivity.

Birth colors, flowers, herbs, and gemstones

BIRTH HERBS

Much of the modern world's knowledge of the zodiac comes to it via generations of gypsy lore, which is also rich in herbal remedies for many of our human ailments. In gypsy culture, Earth (de Develski) is the Divine Mother of all existence, the supreme deity for these people who live an outdoor life at one with nature, who use a secret sign language sourced in their knowledge of leaves and grasses, and who can whistle the birds right out of the trees.

Gypsies believe that the earth's abundant life forms throb to a shared life force, the power of the universe. They believe the rhythm of other planets, whirling and pulsating in their courses, are at one with ours.

Nicolas Culpeper, England's seventeenth-century herbalist and astrologer, shared this philosophy. He assigned to each herb its ruling planet and dealt with each according to its zodiac character, be that impulsive Aries, restless Sagittarius or tenacious Scorpio. He wrote:

"Let the planet that governs the herb be angular and the stronger the better. If they can, in herbs of Saturn, let Saturn be the ascendant; in the herbs of Mars, let Mars be in the mid-heaven, for in those houses, they delight. Let the moon apply to them by good aspect and let her not be in the houses of her enemies."

Astrological signs and their herbs
ARIES • Horseradish, marjoram, rosemary, garlic
TAURUS • Mint, tansy, thyme
GEMINI • Dill, caraway, parsley, lavender
CANCER • Lettuce, agrimony, balm, chamomile, cucumber
LEO • Borage, bay, saffron
VIRGO • Fennel, valerian
LIBRA • Dandelion, sweet violets
SCORPIO • Tarragon, basil
SAGITTARIUS • Sage, chervil
CAPRICORN • Comfrey, fumitory (bleeding heart)
AQUARIUS • Elder flowers, barley
PISCES • Rose hip, lungwort

BIRTH FLOWERS

JANUARY • *Carnation* • To those born in January, the well-loved carnation promises a life of variety and empowers them with the quality of courage.

FEBRUARY • *Violet* • As a birth flower, the violet symbolizes the gentle qualities of modesty and shyness, along with strength of character in adversity.

MARCH • *Daffodil* • The spiritually uplifting daffodil bestows dignity and chivalry on those born in March, the earliest month of the Northern Hemisphere's springtime in which it first blooms.

APRIL • *Sweet pea* • Along with grace and a sense of delicacy, the sweet pea brings with it the possibility of a varied life for the versatile April-born.

MAY • *Lily of the valley* • Lily of the valley is a very auspicious birth flower. It symbolizes happiness, joy, optimism, and bright, new beginnings throughout life.

JUNE • *Rose* • Love is the magnificent birth gift of the rose, representing aspects of love: rosebuds signifying unawakened love and yellow roses jealousy.

JULY • *Larkspur or Delphinium* • Named for the irrepressible dolphin (from the Greek *delphis*), the blooming delphinium bestows health and a talent for happiness on those born in July.

AUGUST • *Poppy* • The poppy's many blessings are a capacity for renewal, an understanding that there's a time for every purpose: beauty, grief, loyalty, and courage.

SEPTEMBER • *Aster* • Grace, modesty, and a sweetness of disposition are bestowed on those given the stylish aster that is considered emblematic of elegance, friendship, and secret love.

OCTOBER • *Calendula or Marigold* • Those born with marigold, follower of the sun, as their mistress are spirited lovers of nature, radiating happiness to all around them.

NOVEMBER • *Chrysanthemum* • The chrysanthemum symbolizes perfection, which is often expressed as the well-balanced philosophies of life practiced by those who call it their birth flower.

DECEMBER • *Holly* • Holly, emblematic of physical and spiritual renewal, bestows the gifts of foresight, strength, and resilience on those who are born in December.

BIRTH GEMSTONES

ARIES • *Diamond* • The diamond is the emblem of fearlessness and invincibility, a fine choice for self-expressive, enterprising, impatient Aries, endowing them with extraordinary courage and strength.

TAURUS • *Emerald* • The emerald, which is in astrological harmony with the typically straightforward, truth-loving Taureans, was much used in divining the future and to reveal the truth in any situation.

GEMINI • *Moonstone* • The generally sensitive, complex, faithful, and romantic Geminis are represented by these translucent gems.

CANCER • *Carnelian* • Carnelians range in color from bright red to a warm honey color. The bright red ones are said to appease anger, while honey-colored carnelians are said to exhilarate the soul and banish fear.

LEO • *Sardonyx* • The sardonyx, symbolizing dignity, is highly compatible with the characteristically kingly instincts of those born under the sign of the Lion.

VIRGO • *Sapphire* • The sapphire symbolizes nobility, virtue, justice, and loyalty, qualities in harmony with Virgo's quest for perfection in themselves and others. The sapphire attracts divine favor and protects its wearers from envy and harm.

LIBRA • *Opal* • Opals vary widely in popularity and acceptance. Opals are said to guard their wearers against lightning strikes and are also thought to cheer the heart and mind.

SCORPIO • *Topaz* • Whatever their color, topazes symbolize cheerfulness and are reputedly able to ward off danger, nervous ailments, nightmares, and violent passions. They also help restore sight and augment the wealth of their wearers.

SAGITTARIUS • *Turquoise* • Charming turquoise is the symbol of luck and love—a perfect stone for the typical Sagittarian, who is notoriously lucky and likable, despite being simultaneously romantic, freedom-loving, and ethical.

CAPRICORN • *Garnet* • Emblematic of constancy and fidelity, the garnet is true to the Capricorn instinct to be always rational yet faithful and devoted.

AQUARIUS • *Amethyst* • Amethysts, symbolizing sobriety and temperance, are highly compatible with the Aquarian temperament: friendly, popular, but also idealistic, self-reliant, and reliable.

PISCES • *Aquamarine* • The delicate and translucent aquamarine is the symbol of elegance.

BIRTH COLORS

ARIES • *Red* • Red contains energy to equal the typically forceful temperament of those born under Aries. This color is used to counter negative thinking and to improve vitality.

TAURUS • *Pink* • A color helpful in reducing the effects of stress, pink symbolizes romantic love and generally encourages sympathetic feelings between people.

GEMINI • *Yellow* • Yellow represents the nervous system, which is said to stimulate and strengthen. A yellow room is an ideal choice for generally optimistic, energetic, versatile, and creatively self-expressive Geminis.

CANCER • *Violet* • Violet is the most spiritual color in the spectrum, the one most likely to trigger mental relaxation and meditation, well suited to the sensitive, persistent, deep-thinking, and introspective Cancerians.

LEO • *Orange* • Orange most accurately reflects the fiery and powerful Leo personality and inspires achievement. Strong, stimulating, rich, and packed with positive vibrations, orange is a beneficial choice for big-hearted Leos.

VIRGO • *Brown* • A rich, warm brown, a color symbolic of the soil and nurturing, helps reassure and calm self-doubting or distressed Virgoans.

LIBRA • *Indigo* • Librans are generally friendly people, fond of harmony. Cool indigo blue, which emanates gentle vibrations, is their lucky color.

SCORPIO • *Black* • Powerful black brings luck to the strongly individual and independent Scorpio personality. Wearing black, they are being true to the Scorpion's secretive natures.

SAGITTARIUS • *Light Blue* • Pale blue, symbolizing clarity, enhances the powers of forward-looking Sagittarians.

CAPRICORN • *Green* • The balance and harmony vibrations of cool and soothing green complement the systematic Capricornian approach to life and promote peace within for the restless, ever-striving Capricornians.

AQUARIUS • *Royal Blue* • Naturally dignified, active, independent, thoughtful, and creative, Aquarians are well stimulated and complemented by the clear, tranquil and refreshing vibrations of royal blue.

PISCES • *Aquamarine* • Aquamarine, simultaneously blue, green, and turquoise, both invites and defies definition.

YOUR PERSONALIZED CHART

How to make your personalized chart

Your birthday is the key to your personality and your life path. This dictionary will let you gather all the information you need to help you understand all of the influences of your birth date.

YOUR BIRTHDAY BY THE HOUR

In Chinese astrology, you will find your hour of birth reveals aspects of your hidden self and secret passions. This is called the ascendant sign.

• If you know your hour of birth, check the table on page 11.
• The animal of Chinese astrology that corresponds with the hour of your birth:

EXAMPLE If you were born between 1 P.M. and 3 P.M., your hour of birth corresponds with the Sheep. Look in the A–Z section (from page 48) for what your corresponding animal reveals about you.

EXAMPLE If you correspond to the Sheep, turn to pages 150–151 to learn that your secret to success is your ability to adapt.

ABOUT MY ASCENDANT SIGN

YOUR BIRTHDAY BY THE DAY

In various astrological systems, your day of birth can reveal many aspects of your personality. Look at the table on pages 12–27 for information about your day of birth and then turn to the A–Z section from page 48 to find out more information about your birthday. The table is organized so that each day in a year reveals the following information:

- Western zodiac sign
- Color
- Food
- Flowers
- Herbs
- Gemstones

EXAMPLE If you were born on March 27, you are an Aries. Turn to pages 54–57 to learn more about what being an Aries means.

- Native American birth time animal totem
- Native American seasonal element

EXAMPLE If you were born in the Northern Hemisphere on March 27, you are also a Hawk in Native American astrology. Turn to pages 96–97 to learn more about the Hawk. In Native American astrology, it is believed that each person also corresponds to a seasonal element, which can be one of four key elements—Earth, Air, Fire, or Water. If you were born on March 27, you are linked with the element of Fire. Turn to pages 86–87 to learn how Fire affects your life and personality.

YOUR BIRTHDAY BY THE MONTH

In Chinese astrology, the month of your birth corresponds to your love life. Turn to the table on pages 28–29 and find the corresponding animal sign for your love life. Turn to the A–Z section from page 48 to find out what your animal sign reveals about your character in intimate relationships.

EXAMPLE If you were born in September, your love life animal sign would be the Rooster. Turn to pages 134–135 for more information about the Rooster animal sign.

YOUR BIRTHDAY BY THE YEAR

In Chinese astrology, the year of your birth corresponds with your dominant sign, which gives you information about your distinctive personality traits. Turn to the table on pages 31–33 to find what animal sign corresponds with your year of birth. The table also tells you which of the five key elements in Chinese astrology—Wood, Fire, Earth, Metal, or Water—corresponds to your year of birth.

EXAMPLE If you were born on March 27, 1956, you will find that your dominant animal sign is the Monkey (turn to pages 110–111 for more information about the Monkey animal sign) and that your dominant element is Fire. See pages 84–85 for what the Fire element means in Chinese astrology.

YOUR LUCKY BIRTH NUMBER

A simple calculation for working out your birth number, which is the addition of all the numbers (day, month and year) of your birthday to come up with a single digit number (or some special double-digit numbers) and which can 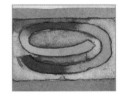 provide some surprising insights into your life and personality. See pages 34–35 to find out how to calculate your birth number. Then turn to the A–Z section (from page 48) to read about what your number means to you.

EXAMPLE If you were born on March 29, 1963, your lucky birth number is thirty-three. Look at pages 162–163 for more information about what this lucky number means to you.

> You can now use the template on the next three pages to make your own summary of your birthday profile. The profile leaves you space to insert keywords gathered from the A–Z section (from page 48) of this dictionary.

A template for your full birthday profile

PROFILE DETAILS

NAME: _____

DATE OF BIRTH: _____

TIME OF BIRTH: _____

CHINESE ASTROLOGY

Your dominant sign (by the year): _____

Key words from the A–Z section: _____

_____

_____

_____

Your corresponding element (Wood, Fire, Earth, Metal, Water): ____

Key words from the A–Z section: _____

_____

_____

_____

Your love sign (by the month): _____

Key words from the A–Z section: _____

_____

_____

_____

Your ascendant sign or your secret self (by the hour): _____

Key words from the A–Z section: _____

_____

_____

_____

Look at the mix of animal signs. What does it mean? _____

_____

_____

_____

_____

_____

_____

EXAMPLE If you were born on November 29, 1963, your dominant sign is a Rabbit (corresponding with the element of Wood), your ascendant sign is a Dragon (Earth), and your love sign is a Pig (Water), your mix of animal signs indicate that you have a comprehensive array of character traits. The Dragon ascendant ensures you have strength and willpower when they are needed.

Look at the mix of elements. What does it mean?

_____

_____

_____

_____

EXAMPLE If your dominant sign corresponds with the element of Wood, your ascendant sign with Earth, and your love sign with Water, your mix of elements is positive, harmonious, and centered on the softer, more creative elements of Wood and Water. As there is no Fire or Metal present, you are quite easygoing and artistic, but you also have a practical, realistic mindset because of the influence of Earth.

WESTERN ASTROLOGY

Your zodiac sign:
_____

Key words from the A–Z section:
_____

_____

_____

_____

Your favorite or lucky items:
_____

_____

Color: _____

Food: _____

Flowers: _____

Herbs: _____

Gemstones: _____

NATIVE AMERICAN ASTROLOGY

Corresponding birth time totem animal: _____

Key words from the A–Z section: _____
_____
_____
_____

Corresponding birth time element (Earth, Air, Fire, Water): _____

Key words from the A–Z section: _____
_____
_____
_____

Corresponding elemental clan: _____

Key words from the A–Z section: _____
_____
_____
_____

Corresponding season: _____

Key words from the A–Z section: _____
_____
_____
_____

Corresponding seasonal element: _____

Key words from the A–Z section: _____
_____
_____
_____

Corresponding seasonal totem animal: _____

Key words from the A–Z section: _____
_____
_____

YOUR LUCKY BIRTH NUMBER

Your lucky birth number: _____

Key words from the A–Z section: _____
_____
_____
_____
_____

Discovering who you are: Combining East and West

You may be aware of your sign of the zodiac in Western astrology, but you may not necessarily know your sign for the other types of astrology discussed in this book.

Unfortunately, the sources of ancient wisdom do not always agree as to the dates when each sign changes. Also, as many of the systems are lunar, they may not line up exactly from one year to the next. The answer, for those who find themselves on the cusp of any sign in any type of astrology, is to read both the signs that are close to your birthday.

However, there is a way of blending the various astrological systems that will enable you to arrive at quite a comprehensive and integrated character analysis. Such a combined profile could identify the unique subtleties that may help accurately determine your communication style and, therefore, possibilities for relationship and career success.

While Chinese, Western, and animal totem astrology systems differ, there are some key similarities:

- Each system has twelve core signs, often represented by an animal.
- Each system divides the twelve signs into four groups of three.
- Each system relies on elements (Earth, Fire, Water, Air, Wood, and Metal in Chinese astrology and Earth, Air, Fire, and Water in Western and animal totem astrology) to reveal the differences between members of each animal sign, as well as commonalities between signs.

Here are some of the fundamental differences.

THE CHINESE SYSTEM

This is based on a sixty-year "life cycle," within which the twelve animal signs, along with one of the five elements, rules for one whole lunar year: 12 signs x 5 elements = 60.

One of the five Chinese elements governs the core traits of each animal sign (this is sometimes referred to as the primary element). Each animal sign is also influenced by the year of birth (see table on pages 31–33).

THE WESTERN ZODIAC

This zodiac is based on the solar year, where each sign rules for approximately thirty days of the 365-day year. Each sign is associated with only one primary element, of which there are four.

COMBINING THE SYSTEMS, STEP BY STEP

1 Add your Western and animal totem sign traits and the associated element characteristics to those of your dominant Chinese animal sign.

2 Note the energy type of both your Chinese animal (yin or yang) and Western and animal totem sign (masculine or feminine; active or receptive).

3 Look for similarities and contrasts among all the traits. Are specific traits heightened as a result, or are they more varied?

4 Determine if a balance is achieved between the two types of energies.

Chinese	Western	Animal totem
Yang	Masculine/positive	Active
Yin	Feminine/negative	Receptive

5 Do the elements vary or does one dominate? How do the characteristics of the elements influence your animal traits?

EXAMPLE

Oprah Winfrey, talk show host, born January 29, 1954.

Profile	Sign	Element	Energy
Chinese profile	Snake	Fire	Yin
Western profile	Aquarius	Air	Masculine/positive
Animal totem profile	Otter	Air	Active

SUMMARY OF COMBINED PROFILES

In Oprah's combined profile, the energy is tending toward an active, extroverted form. The relationship between the elements of fire and air are productive, with air fanning the flames of fire. The emphasis on the element of air corresponds to a heightened intellectual and intuitive ability. Aquarian snakes are ruled by their minds and make for deep and original thinkers who are skilled at sensing the mood in any situation and are able to respond appropriately. Both snakes and Aquarians are great observers and like to take an unbiased and objective approach to life. Otters are a pure sign of air, emphasizing high intelligence and a strong psychic ability.

A

AIR

In many Native American belief systems, Fire, Water, Air, and Earth are the four elements considered the most important natural forces. They permeate every aspect of life, ensuring that living things go through a recurring process of birth, life, death, and regeneration. The different elements also cause differences in personality, highlighting particular strengths and weaknesses of character. The elements are also the foundation of many other aspects of the natural world. The following table outlines the correspondences of Air.

WHO AM I?

KEY ATTRIBUTES	Communication, intelligence, renewal, thought, logic
AREAS GOVERNED BY THE ELEMENT	The mind and the psyche
SEASON OF LIFE IT GOVERNS	Winter
DIRECTION	North
TIME OF DAY IT GOVERNS	Night
TIME OF LIFE IT GOVERNS	Old age (60 years plus)
ANIMAL BIRTH TOTEM	Deer: 5/21–6/20 (N); 11/22–12/21 (S) Otter: 1/20–2/18 (N); 7/23–8/22 (S) Raven: 9/23–10/22 (N); 3/21–4/19 (S)
ANIMAL SEASONAL TOTEM	Otter, Snow Goose, Wolf

We are all affected by two elements influencing our character and behavior at any one time—the element of the birth time animal totem and the element of the seasonal animal totem. If the two elements and their key attributes are taken into account when analyzing each animal totem's character, a more detailed and accurate description of that totem will be gained.

AIR AS BIRTH TIME ELEMENT

The instinctive behavior of each birth time animal totem is influenced by the birth time element. It is this element that creates the foundation of each animal totem's basic nature—the essence of who you are. Animal totems with Air as their birth time element are the otter (see pages 116–117), Deer (see pages 70–71), and Raven (see pages 132–133).

With Air as their birth time element, these animal totems all have keen intellects and inquiring minds. Otter, Deer, and Raven people tend to operate using logic and rational thought. They are clever individuals with psychic abilities.

AIR AS SEASONAL ELEMENT

The seasonal animal totem provides additional gifts and qualities. These qualities relate to the totems' inner senses, spiritual endeavors, and general behavior. The animal totems with Air as their seasonal element are the Snow Goose, Otter, and Wolf. They

have the force of Air directing their behavior. People born during this time usually show good verbal expression and logic. They are thoughtful, reflective, wise, independent, and people oriented. They are highly intelligent and have active minds. As they like to take time out to rejuvenate, their best time is the night. Sleep brings them rest, and their dreams bring them powerful messages and lessons about life.

The winter time animal totem is the White Buffalo. The White Buffalo was a rare animal, sacred to Native Americans, as it would sacrifice itself totally for the well being of humans. The Buffalo was believed to be the messenger of knowledge in spiritual union with the Creator of the World.

PURE SIGNS

The Otter is the pure Air sign (Air of Air). People of the Otter totem reflect the attributes of air more than any other animal totem. This means their minds are acutely developed, they are highly intelligent, and they have particularly strong psychic powers. With such attributes, Otter people are challenged more than any other sign to seek balance regularly with the earth, to ensure they remain practical and grounded in their everyday lives.

AQUARIUS

BIRTH DATES: January 22 to February 20

WHO AM I?

SYMBOL	The water carrier The volume of intuitive knowledge Aquarius holds
QUEST	Illumination
RULING PLANET	Uranus Individuality, freedom, independence, innovation
RULING ELEMENT	Air Intelligence, articulateness, objectivity, idealism
POLARITY	Positive Impulsivity, excitability, communicativeness
QUALITY	Fixed Stability, loyalty, endurance
COLOR	Royal blue Can help restore self-confidence and increase levels of mental and physical energy
FOOD	Almonds, beets, caraway, hazelnuts, endives
FLOWER	Carnations, violets, holly
HEALING HERB	Elder flower Soothing for Aquarians suffering from nervous tension
GEMSTONE	Amethyst Symbolizes sobriety and temperance
SUITABLE GIFTS	Jewelry featuring amethysts, fossils, and jet; vases; and decorative bowls for floating candles

TEMPERAMENT

Those born under the sign of Aquarius are valiant and self-confident, yet blessed by the absence of arrogance. Being highly independent, they like doing things their own way, but they can always be swayed by a logical argument. Aquarians tend to have their own notion of time and find it difficult to conform to rules and set procedures.

Typically, Aquarians are adventurers but they are not foolhardy, tending to assess every aspect of a situation carefully. They are keen to avoid exceeding personal limitations, either financial, physical, or psychological. While eager to discover fresh pastures, they are also reliable. They can deal with emergencies, remaining calm.

Aquarians are quite unlikely to be spoiled by material success. They are blessed with a temperament that allows them to enjoy whatever they have. Greed and power-lust are not usually part of their character. In later life, Aquarians often turn to work associated with improving the welfare of others and may use their innate powers of communication, which have often been well honed in their early to mid-life careers.

Aquarians are an interesting emotional mixture. Their watery element can mean that they are oversensitive and inclined to respond with excessive or inappropriate emotion on occasions. However, they usually have the gift of intuition, which is specifically evident in their ability to anticipate or tune into other people's thoughts and feelings.

Aquarians born on or around January 27 are the most sensitive of all. They may have to be coaxed out of their safety zone if they are ever to come into contact with the harsher world beyond. Those born on or around February 2 may be gifted with psychic power, which will emerge in its own time.

Personal areas that Aquarians may need to develop include working on emotional involvement, productivity, and the ability to perform within constraints.

LOVE AND FRIENDSHIP

Aquarians are usually popular, the archetypal good friends. They enjoy people individually or in groups. Indeed, the Aquarian view of the world is truly global, and one of the Aquarian's characteristic interests is helping to bring about world change. In their daily lives, Aquarians invariably demonstrate an ability to win the trust and friendship of very difficult people.

Their personal style, usually quite distinctive and very pleasing to many people, is the manifestation of their personal magnetism.

Those born on February 6 can be especially dazzling, with a sparkling, keen mind and an appealing, cheerful nature. Although they appreciate the input other people can provide in both a personal and professional sense, they tend to tackle all activities single-handed.

Ideally, Aquarians should seek partners who can exert restraint without either driving them to rebellious excess or suppressing their love of adventure. It is important the partner has a spirit of adventure and a zest for living, because a too-timorous attitude will only irritate headstrong Aquarians and possibly spur them into action they may not otherwise have taken.

Aquarians will enjoy a companion who is quick-minded and versatile, has common sense, and is very handy at organizing situations, very supportive, and unlikely to oppose the Aquarian's more realistic projects. While Aquarians are not moody as a rule, those born on or near January 29 can be secretive. These Aquarians in particular will be happiest with a partner who is cheerful and unconditionally affectionate.

Aquarians should choose friends and business associates with care. Their sensitive natures will always expose them to the influence of others in quite subtle but nevertheless significant ways.

WORK AND BUSINESS

Aquarians are hardworking in their professional lives. Though they are not fickle, they may experience more than their share of job and career changes. This may be particularly so during middle life, when a whole new avenue may appear. It is also fairly typical for Aquarians to become involved in more than one business venture at a time. This situation may grow naturally out of semiprofessional hobbies, for instance, or may be deliberately sought by Aquarians who wish to take on more work in order to create more personal and financial profit in their lives.

Aquarians often have the enviable gift of being able to express a very creative mind through exceptional manual dexterity. Aquarians are also most likely to be blessed with excellent financial sense, so they have an enormous range of choice across the spectrum of professions relying on financial skills.

At work, Aquarians are often perceived as aloof and rather eccentric, as they can become preoccupied with the ideas racing through their heads. They need an emotionally stable and noise-free environment, free of complex regulations and politics, in order to feel comfortable and to release their powers of innovation.

They need an occupation that challenges their intellect, and sufficient freedom and time to devise innovative plans and think of offbeat ideas. Aquarians are drawn to jobs that involve problem solving and analysis rather than routine work. They are usually attracted to science and the arts, and flourish as scientists, writers, inventors, or engineers. They are also happy to work in areas involving new technology, electronics, and humanitarian causes.

Until they find their niche, Aquarians can be restless and unsettled, and this can create open conflict and antagonism toward management. Aquarians are not generally attracted to leadership positions. They lack respect for the many policies and procedures inherent in the role and will take a minimal role in sorting out human relations issues.
Their contribution is their forward-thinking, relaxed approach. Those falling under their responsibility will be highly stimulated, encouraged to contribute ideas and solutions, and provided with the necessary freedom and technology to make this happen.

BLENDING THE SYSTEMS

Aquarians born in January

January Aquarians are independent and self-reliant, with a keen intellect and an interest in a wide range of topics. The Chinese Ox sign adds much-needed practicality and a hardworking element, while the receptive Earth element gives them a keen eye for what looks good and the ability to find ingenious solutions for difficult projects. The Native American Otter of the Butterfly clan makes Aquarians clever, bold, playful, and helpful, and it gives them a delightful sense of humor and a clear and logical mind.

Aquarians born in February

February Aquarians have a talent for arbitration and communication and the courage to stick to their guns. The Chinese sign of the active Wood Tiger is responsible for their sparkling personality, magnetic looks, and sense of humor. The active Wood element encourages them to make a success out of their own interests, but it is hard for them to work for others. The Native American Otter of the Butterfly clan ensures that they are logical, humorous, and fun to be with. These Aquarians make sympathetic friends and respected and honored bosses.

ARIES

●

BIRTH DATES: March 21 to April 20

WHO AM I?

SYMBOL	*The Ram* The Arian's impulsive and forceful approach to life
QUEST	*Initiation*
RULING PLANET	*Mars* As the Ram, an impulsive and forceful approach to life
RULING ELEMENT	*Fire* Enthusiasm, confidence, passion, and energy
POLARITY	*Positive* Impulsivity, excitability, communicativeness, and sociability
QUALITY	*Cardinal* Spontaneity, restlessness, desire for action
COLOR	*Red* Can be used to counter negative thinking and improve vitality
FOOD	*Artichoke, asparagus, chili, garlic, coriander, carrots*
FLOWER	*Daffodil, sweet pea*
HEALING HERB	*Garlic, horseradish, lavender, marjoram, and rosemary* Herbs ruled by the planets Mars and Mercury
GEMSTONE	*Diamond* The emblem of fearlessness and invincibility
SUITABLE GIFTS	Diamond necklace and jewelry featuring bloodstone, rubies, or garnets; candles; chocolates

TEMPERAMENT

Some Arians come across as loud, while others are quiet and reserved; either way, they never allow the grass to grow under their feet. Aries is the first sign of the zodiac and represents eternal youth. No matter their age, Arians have endless reserves of energy, and loads of enthusiasm and curiosity. They propel themselves headfirst into the world each day with no fear or reservations. With their sights planted clearly ahead, Arians have little respect for tradition or convention, and this can sometimes create friction. Passionate, fearless, and impulsive, Arians are often attracted to reckless activities and hair-raising adventures.

Arians born around March 21 tend to be warm-hearted as well as ambitious. Not only are they keen to seek opportunities for advancement, they are especially attracted to fresh, unexplored fields in which to seek their fortune.

Arians are highly individualistic, sometimes quite topsy-turvy in their approach to life, but usually hardworking. Compromise does not come easily to them and they are impatient. They may also be quick-tempered and sharp-tongued. They are competitive both at work and in their hobbies, and they can gain a high position in life through a combination of diligent work and adroit political skills.

Arians are keen on art and music, and as they tend to be emotional as well as highly communicative, they may also do very well in the performing arts. Their strengths as communicators may mean they have a talent for telepathy or clairvoyance. Some may have the gift of prophecy, dreaming of events before they come to pass.

Preferring to follow their instincts rather than sticking to the facts, Arians are great ones for acting on hunches. They will not usually shine at matters involving facts or figures, such as statistics or note-taking. Arian energy will probably reap material rewards and riches in early to middle life, and so it is Arians who often, after retirement from the world of business or professional practice, guide the fortunes of benevolent institutions.

Personal areas that Arians may need to develop include learning how to compromise, how to empathize, and how to use their judgment wisely.

LOVE AND FRIENDSHIP

Passion rules Arians, in terms of love and sex and also in terms of what they believe to be important. They try hard in marriage and love their children deeply. Arians thrive in relationships with partners who can help to implement their ambitious plans and are

towers of strength in tough times; however, Arians are usually strong enough to survive any mismatch. More often than not, they will fulfill most of their potential, no matter what the nature of their personal or professional partnerships.

A quietly systematic partner who is patient and adaptable will help the fiery Aries in life. The ideal partner for those born under the sign of the Ram is someone who has a generous nature and is able to overlook the odd slight or moment of rudeness when the Arian is extremely brusque, for instance when intent on finishing a job.

Arians tend to ask a great deal of themselves and of others. They like to give free rein to their energies and will be happiest among friends who are not daunted by their ardent, sometimes forceful natures. Not everyone can keep up with a determined Arian!

WORK AND BUSINESS

At work, Arians are highly competitive and driven; they are big-picture people who are quick to create action plans and initiate projects. Goal-oriented and reward-focused, Arians are easily motivated to excel. They make forceful change agents. They often excel at effective presentation and so make good salespeople—preferably of a single product—because Arians are usually at their best when narrowing their focus.

Arians need constant challenge and frequent change in their work environments if they are to stay stimulated. They are at their best in difficult situations that require quick decision making and

 action. Whatever their endeavors, however, Arians need space to move and the ability to set their own agenda and pace.

Typically, Arians are involved in very positive and productive occupations that include the laying of foundations or building in some way. Architecture, engineering, education, and philanthropic pursuits all fall within the ambit of the Arian disposition. Arians can also become professional athletes, corporate executives, entrepreneurs, and firefighters. They may also display an interest in working with fire or metal.

Arians make demanding and motivating leaders. Their competitive streak means they will rarely recognize or accept defeat, and they are prone to setting unrealistic expectations for themselves and others. On the up side, the Aries boss leads by example and is openly appreciative of others' initiative and hard work. You will always know where you stand with your very direct and frank Aries boss.

World leaders are frequently drawn from Arian ranks. Outwardly confident, active and energetic, ambitious, and curious,

Arians can also suffer from stress and frustration. Not surprisingly, the head is the body part most often afflicted in Aries people. When their ceaseless daily activity gets too much even for energetic Arians and their heads hurt from all that ramlike head-butting or they are feeling distressed by life, bring on the herbs ruled by the

planets Mars (named for the Roman god of war) and Mercury (the winged messenger of Roman mythology), such as garlic, horseradish, marjoram and rosemary.

BLENDING THE SYSTEMS

Arians born in March

The active, energetic Fire sign of Aries suggests that March Arians can rush in head first where angels fear to tread. Arians are honest, humorous, and kind, but they can be so focused on their goals that they walk over others while achieving them. The Chinese sign is the Rabbit, which gives a touch of class and a need for close personal relationships; the receptive Wood element can involve Arians in causes. The Native American sign of the Red Hawk gives Arians energy and makes them dangerous people with which to disagree. The Hawk's farsightedness also enables Arians to make a success of their ideas.

Arians born in April

The extroverted Fire sign of Aries gives April Arians great courage and optimism, and they get things done. The honest, humorous, and outspoken nature of Aries is echoed by the Dragon of Chinese astrology which, being active and linked with the earth, enables them to build for the future and lead others. The Native American Red Hawk of the Thunderbird clan makes them friendly and generous, as well as strong and capable leaders. This totem animal changes on the last day of the sign to the Beaver of the Turtle clan, which is slower to act and keen to improve the environment.

B

BEAVER

BIRTH DATES: Northern Hemisphere: April 20 to May 20
Southern Hemisphere: October 23 to November 21

WHO AM I?

BIRTH TIME ANIMAL TOTEM	Beaver
BIRTH TIME ELEMENT	Earth
ELEMENTAL CLAN	Turtle
ENERGY FLOW	Receptive
LIFE PATH	To embrace emotions readily and express them constantly, thus avoiding a totally logical approach to life
PERSONAL GIFTS	Tenacity, practicality, steadfastness, industriousness, patience, reliability, dexterity
PERSONAL CHALLENGES	Overindulgence, stubbornness, being overly opinionated, inflexibility
CORRESPONDING SEASON	The heart of spring—a time of rapid growth
SEASONAL ELEMENT	Fire
SEASONAL TOTEM	Eagle
COLOR	Blue
PLANT	Lily
GEMSTONE	Turquoise

BEAVER PEOPLE

Native Americans view Beavers as nature's prime example of industriousness. Beaver dams are engineering feats, cleverly created to provide the animals with many entries and exits so that they are secure from enemies.

Beaver people are extremely practical, hardworking individuals who demonstrate an almost unlimited abundance of patience, whether at work on individual tasks or in the company of others.

Beavers expect high standards of performance from themselves and others. Yet they are not stressed by deadlines, as they apply themselves methodically and commit others to a clear action plan that will get everyone there in the end. Beavers are extremely task-focused, operating at the material level. Hence, they do not come across as big talkers, travelers, or socializers.

Beavers' families and homes are extremely important to them. They will readily commit whatever is required—money, time, or anything else—to make the hearth secure.

Beavers' energy type is reflective, which means they like to think before they act. They have the capacity to embrace the emotional, nurturing side of life; Beavers do feel deeply about their lives and the people in them. However, they can have a difficult time expressing and demonstrating their feelings.

ELEMENTAL CLAN

As their birth time element is Earth, Beavers belong to the Turtle clan. The turtle is one of the oldest surviving animals on earth today. It is also one of the most harmonious. Its ability to use the earth and sun for laying its eggs and hatching its young while it lives predominantly in the water demonstrates the balance it has achieved among the elements. Like the turtle, Beaver people are grounded, stable, and secure. They are loyal and act according to their strong values and principles. They are very practical, constructive, and industrious. Just like their element, they can be nurturing and sustaining to those around them. They will only be of value to themselves and others if they learn to accommodate the qualities of all the other elements—Fire, Air, and Water.

SEASONAL ELEMENT

Your seasonal totem animal, the Eagle, is closely related to the element governing the season in which you were born. For more information about your seasonal totem animal and your seasonal element, Fire, see pages 86–87.

• *Strengths to cultivate* Responsibility and accountability, self-sacrifice, diligence, a sensible nature • *Possible weaknesses to address* Stubbornness, an authoritative approach when dealing with others, intolerance toward others' views and beliefs

BROWN BEAR

BIRTH DATES: Northern Hemisphere: August 23 to September 22
Southern Hemisphere: February 19 to March 20

WHO AM I?

BIRTH TIME ANIMAL TOTEM	Brown bear
BIRTH TIME ELEMENT	Earth
ELEMENTAL CLAN	Turtle
ENERGY FLOW	Receptive
LIFE PATH	To provide space in your life to nurture the spiritual core and, in the process, achieve the ultimate—balance between the physical, emotional, and spiritual planes
PERSONAL GIFTS	Perseverance, judgment, fairness and justice, powers of discrimination, responsibility, common sense, courage, wisdom
PERSONAL CHALLENGES	Cynicism, critical nature, aloofness, conventionalism
CORRESPONDING SEASON	Late summer—harvesting time, a time to reap what has been sown
SEASONAL ELEMENT	Water
SEASONAL TOTEM	Coyote
COLOR	Purple
PLANT	Violet
GEMSTONE	Amethyst

BROWN BEAR PEOPLE

The sheer size and strength of Brown Bears provides them with much magnetism and presence. Native Americans have due respect for the Brown Bear, admiring its hunting skills and the strong protection it gives its young.

Brown bear people at their best are hardworking, discerning, and tenacious. They often demonstrate good judgment in their decision making, as well as fairness and consideration when dealing with others. Where there is a problem, when someone is in distress or even just when something is broken, Brown Bear people feel it their responsibility to fix it all. In fact, they may have the talent of being able to fix just about anything.

Like their animal totem, Brown Bear people have a strong physical presence. They attract the attention of others with their courage to stand up for what they believe is fair and just, and they make protective and loyal friends, family members, and colleagues.

Their particular gifts lie in their considered approach to life and in their perseverance. Seeing a Brown Bear person triumph through a difficult time is a pure vision of perseverance in action. They are realistic, practical, and analytical people who demonstrate good sense and self-reliance. Brown bear people can rise to meet any challenge.

While they are at their best in the physical world, Brown Bear people also have a natural tie to the world of the heart and their emotions. So, as well as being physically magnificent, Brown Bear people are at the same time gentle, warm, caring, cheerful, and good-natured.

ELEMENTAL CLAN

As their birth time element is Earth, Brown Bears belong to the Turtle clan. The turtle is one of the oldest surviving animals on earth today. It is also one of the most harmonious. Its ability to use the earth and sun for laying its eggs and hatching its young while it lives predominantly in the water demonstrates the balance it has achieved among the elements.

Like the turtle, Brown Bear people are grounded, stable, and secure. They are loyal and act according to their strong values and principles. They are very practical, constructive, and industrious. Just like their element, they can be nurturing and sustaining to those around them. They will only be of value to themselves and others if they learn to accommodate the qualities of all the other elements—Fire, Air, and Water.

SEASONAL ELEMENT

Your seasonal totem animal, the Coyote, is closely related to the element governing the season in which you were born. For more information about your seasonal totem animal and your seasonal element, Water, see pages 178–179.

• *Strengths to cultivate* Responsibility and accountability, self-sacrifice, a sensible nature, diligence • *Possible weaknesses to address* Stubbornness, authoritative approach when dealing with others, intolerance toward others' views and beliefs

---

CANCER

BIRTH DATES: June 22 to July 22

WHO AM I?

SYMBOL	*The Crab* A hard, protective exterior and vulnerable emotions
QUEST	*Nurturing and protection*
RULING PLANET	*Moon* Emotions, intuition, nurturing, the past
RULING ELEMENT	*Water* Sensitivity, intuitiveness, creativity
POLARITY	*Negative* Receptivity, reserve, the desire for privacy
QUALITY	*Cardinal* Spontaneity, restlessness, orientation toward action
COLOR	*Violet* Can trigger mental relaxation and meditation
FOOD	*Mushrooms, potatoes, cauliflowers, cucumbers, grapes*
FLOWER	*Rose, delphinium, jasmine*
HEALING HERB	*Agronomy, balm, chamomile, cucumber, and lettuce* Herbs ruled by the moon will suit the water element in Cancerians' nature
GEMSTONE	*Carnelian* To exhilarate the soul and banish fear
SUITABLE GIFTS	Jewelry featuring carnelians, moonstones, or sapphires, and gifts for the home, including decorated photograph frames

TEMPERAMENT

Cancerians are among the lucky in life. They seem to be bestowed with health and stamina, personal beauty, charisma, and talents. Their basic nature is cautious and protective. They do not enjoy taking chances and hate the thought of their family being in any kind of trouble. They will fight fiercely for their beliefs.

Many Cancerians are so persistent, they will see a difficult task through to the end rather than abandoning it as a lost cause. They can often withstand trials and tribulations that would destroy others. In any event, given the fortuitous nature of this sign, their setbacks often metamorphose into lucky breaks.

Emotionally, Cancerians share their namesake's thick, protective shell. Where others may lean on friends, partners, or family under duress, they are ultimately loners. Cancerians with birth dates between June 22 and June 25 will find they often are protected during hardship and adversity.

Born under the sign of the Crab, hard outside and soft inside, Cancerians understand that looks can be deceiving, and their intuition serves them well. As they tend to be ethical, they make good detectives, with their instinct for subterfuge, sharp eye for detail, and powers of deduction. Those born around June 29 to 30, often have the gifts of prophetic dreaming and intuitive understanding. Many Cancerians are found among celebrated psychics and hypnotherapists.

Sensitive Cancerians are often very fond of animals and may have quite a menagerie of pets. Farming sheep, cattle, pigs, or poultry are rural pursuits that may appeal to people born under this sign. They also may be interested in or proficient at training animals such as dogs, horses, and even lions!

Personal areas that Cancerians may need to develop include increasing their sense of objectivity, independence, and confidence.

LOVE AND RELATIONSHIPS

Cancerians are slow to fall in love and steadfast once they have done so because they take all relationships seriously. However, they can be somewhat moody and hard to fathom, especially when they feel hurt or upset. A moody Cancerian will appear quite withdrawn and taciturn, debating any dilemma entirely within himself or herself.

Cancer is the sign of nurturing and the family. With an instinctive need to care and to form close emotional ties, Cancerians are skilled at making an extended home and extended family of their workplace and colleagues. Their acute intuition and perception make them adept at reading others' moods and thoughts. They tend to put on a tough, bravado-filled, "no one can hurt me" exterior to shield their super-sensitivity and their vulnerability to life's harsh realities.

Those born under Cancer should seek artistic and original-thinking partners who are fond of company and traveling. Cancerians need stimulating companions, although they are often very private people. They need partners who value a secure home life just as much as they do. Someone with a well-honed sense of the ridiculous, of the comic, will cope best and will even enjoy the wonderfully contradictory elements of the Cancerian partner's personality and behavior.

Cancerians will only form partnerships—personal and business—after careful consideration, usually making their selection alone and without discussion. Once they have made the decision to commit, they usually make loyal, even-tempered partners. Happy 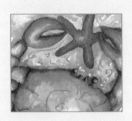 and fulfilled Cancerians love to give enjoyment to their life partners and will often make a special fuss on birthdays and anniversaries.

Cancerians value their individuality and, if this is threatened, quickly retreat from relationships. At some point in their lives, Cancerians are likely to value independence and personal freedom above monetary gain or other's opinions of them.

WORK AND BUSINESS

Cancerians have a responsible and sensible attitude to their working life, often choosing a job that puts them in touch with the public. They are individualists who like to entertain, amuse, or in some creative way give pleasure to others. They are also renowned as naturally competitive, extraordinarily hardworking people who always produce the desired result. They excel as skilled public speakers and find satisfying jobs in public relations, sales, travel, and hospitality. They have a particular talent for making others feel safe and comfortable and make excellent social workers and counselors.

As they are ambitious, responsible, methodical, and sticklers for detail, Cancerians may reach the highest levels of government or community service. They often gravitate toward philanthropic work and have a strong sense of social justice.

A harmonious and close-knit work environment is essential for Cancerians' well-being. Insecurity plagues them at the best of times and requires active management, particularly during times of change.

Cancerians make kind and gentle leaders who expect efficiency and discipline from their staff. They like to create a comfortable and congenial environment where people can work and play together. Soft furnishings, family portraits, and stress balls feature in their work domain. Cancer bosses value and reward cooperation and teamwork.

Responsible, commercially canny Cancerians are contradictory creatures in yet another way—they often handle money strangely. In a vivid and imaginative mood, they will spend too freely, but then may become downright miserly overnight. These swings can be unnerving for business and life partners.

Cancerians may be such introspective worriers that they develop stomach or liver disorders. Eyes, important to observant Cancerians, must also be given special attention. Cancerians should look to herbs ruled by the moon to suit the water element in their nature.

BLENDING THE SYSTEMS

Cancerians born in June

June Cancerians love a full home life, with the members of their family either living with them or constantly in their company. They are also shrewd and cautious business people. When not working, they love to take their families traveling. The Chinese Horse sign is also a great traveler; the active Fire element adds a need for adventure, which, if unfulfilled, can make Cancerians moody or hot-tempered. The Native American sign of the Woodpecker of the Frog clan makes Cancerians affectionate parents who find it hard to let the little ones go when they grow up. Like all Woodpeckers, they enjoy listening to music.

Cancerians born in July

No man or woman is an island, and this is especially true for July Cancerians; they need to have their loved ones around them. Their shrewd common sense and caution make them excellent business people. The Chinese sign of the Goat makes them intuitive, creative, and hardworking, and the receptive Earth element can bring success and leadership in business or the arts. The Native American Woodpecker of the Frog clan can make them a little too dependent upon their partners and desperate for financial and emotional security.

CAPRICORN

●

BIRTH DATES: December 22 to January 21

WHO AM I?

SYMBOL	The Goat Capricorn's ambitious and industrious nature
QUEST	Achievement
RULING PLANET	Saturn Discipline, authority, responsibility, maturity, wisdom
RULING ELEMENT	Earth Practicality, dependability, security, realism
POLARITY	Negative Receptivity, sensitivity, reserve, the desire for privacy
QUALITY	Cardinal Spontaneity, restlessness, the need for action
COLOR	Green Can promote peace within for the restless, ever-striving Capricorn
FOOD	Cheese, beets, tamarind, quince
FLOWER	Holly, carnation, poppy
HEALING HERBS	Comfrey, fumitory
GEMSTONE	Garnet Emblematic of constancy and fidelity
SUITABLE GIFTS	Jewelry featuring garnets, hematite, and onyx; plants for the garden; practical gifts for use in the office, such as a writing set or a set of handy tools

TEMPERAMENT

Some Capricornians are outgoing and happy to be in the limelight, while others are shy and retiring, but all Capricornians are ambitious. Capricorn is the most ambitious and disciplined of all the signs. People born under this sign pursue achievement for practical reasons, rather than for power or control. Their ambitions may be for themselves, their family, their work colleagues, or their country.

Capricornians take life seriously and have a cautious and steady approach. Respectful and dependable, they have a strong sense of duty and are concerned about financial security. Their black-and-white approach to life can sometimes make them dictatorial and moralistic.

Determination and a will to progress onward and upward are hallmarks of this sign. Hard work is no deterrent to Capricornians. Their natural industriousness means they invariably prefer the path of steady advancement. Get-rich-quick schemes have no appeal for them. They would prefer to be sure of arrival by traveling the longer but safer road rather than taking a possibly risky shortcut. They are diligent workers; even very young Capricorn children will often have an exceptional ability, compared with other children of the same age, to focus on a special project.

Capricornians born near the middle of the sign, from January 3 to 5, usually have well developed artistic talents and the qualities of personal magnetism and charisma. Capricornians born toward the beginning of the sign, on or around December 24 or 25, are often good at coming up with fresh solutions to old problems. More usually, however, Capricornians will be the ideal ones to inherit or absorb an idea from someone or somewhere else.

Although Capricornians tend to lack self-confidence, they have the courage to pour their enormous will to succeed into any worthy challenge. Capricornian diligence also tends to create Capricornian good fortune. Their industry is invariably rewarded with flourishing or expanding business. Large and extended families are also typically Capricornian.

Capricornians are very productive people, in all senses of the word. Several marriages are often indicated in their horoscopes.

Of all the signs, Capricornians have the fiercest sense of justice. They simply cannot stand back and observe unfairness of any sort; they will do their best to correct situations like this. Nor do they reserve for others their critical and judgmental capacity. They apply the same strict sense of what is right and what is wrong, particularly what is fair and what is unfair, to their own motives and behavior, and are notoriously hard on themselves—often far harder than they are on others.

Personal areas that Capricornians may need to develop include learning to lighten up, to relax and take time out, to trust in others' abilities, and to play office politics.

LOVE AND RELATIONSHIPS

People relate easily to Capricornians, who are warm and hearty people. Their steadfastness and good heartedness make them attractive as friends and partners.

When happy in a relationship, Capricornians are caring, protective, and very loving. They adore their children, and they are faithful and dependable partners. Capricornians should always seek a partner, notwithstanding their conviction that they can go it alone. The right partner is sometimes the only constant source of peaceful renewal for chronically strife-torn Capricornians. They really need to have someone who is encouraging when life seems too much of an uphill battle, and supportive when they rage against injustice.

They also should seek partners who have an aggressive edge to their personality, who are not afraid of change, and who can confidently counter Capricornian caution when necessary. Partners must also be the kind who will not be intimidated by a Capricornian in a goatishly forthright and self-willed mood.

WORK AND BUSINESS

Capricornians are ambitious and driven. From an early age, they set their sights high on the corporate ladder. They are attracted to power, status, and financial reward, and will work hard to achieve these. They take their responsibilities seriously and readily accept accountability for their actions. They usually like to work alone and at a steady pace, or in a managerial capacity. They have a knack for turning conceptual ideas into practical reality.

Being hard and reliable workers, Capricornians are usually respected and appreciated for what they do, but they can be fussy or demanding. Tending to be disciplined, methodical, and careful in all undertakings, they show considerable talent in accounting, finance and banking, law enforcement, engineering, building, or any mechanical trades.

Capricornians like a structured, traditional work environment where their responsibilities are clearly outlined. Their resistance to change and their attraction to convention make a stable, predictable environment ideal for them. Organizations that offer tenure and career progression suit them.

Capricorn bosses feel quite at home in any management position, enjoying being in control. They make considerate leaders who expect and reward obedience, dedication, and competence. They practice what they preach and are consummate professionals.

BLENDING THE SYSTEMS

Capricornians born in December

The Earth sign of Capricorn means that December Capricornians' ambitions are as much for their families as for themselves. They know that life can be difficult, so they work hard and have a sensible attitude toward money. The Chinese sign of the Rat adds a quiet air that belies the intelligence and determination of people born under this sign. The active Water element ensures they have common sense, a talent for communication, and good business sense. Their Native American sign is the Snow Goose of the Turtle clan, which means the mind roams freely, while the feet are kept firmly on the ground. Capricornians' sensitive feelings can make them see an insult where none is intended.

Capricornians born in January

The Earth sign of Capricorn makes January Capricornians practical, sensible, ambitious, and good to their families. They are less cautious and more interested in art and literature than December Capricornians. Their Chinese Ox sign makes them homebodies with a need for comfort and the good things in life. They are practical and thorough, and they work hard because they fear poverty. The receptive Earth element ensures they are capable and efficient, with an eye for what looks good and what works. The Native American Snow Goose of the Turtle clan signifies a traditional outlook and a regal air, as well as a hard worker with a love of family life.

DEER

BIRTH DATES: Northern Hemisphere: May 21 to June 20
Southern Hemisphere: November 22 to December 21

WHO AM I?

BIRTH TIME ANIMAL TOTEM	Deer
BIRTH TIME ELEMENT	Air
ELEMENTAL CLAN	Butterfly
ENERGY FLOW	Active
LIFE PATH	To take life more seriously when necessary and to focus on preparation and organization in daily life
PERSONAL GIFTS	Grace, gentleness, sensitivity, beauty, versatility, alertness, intuitiveness, wittiness, joviality
PERSONAL CHALLENGES	Nervousness, restlessness, disorganization, over-talkativeness
CORRESPONDING SEASON	Late spring—a time of expansion and flowering, of color and beauty
SEASONAL ELEMENT	Fire
SEASONAL TOTEM	Eagle
COLOR	Green
PLANT	Yarrow
GEMSTONE	Moss agate (a type of quartz)

DEER PEOPLE

Deer are beautiful to behold, something which Native Americans have long esteemed them for, along with their natural grace, gentleness, and agility. To come upon a deer or fawn was a sign for the Native American to stop and appreciate the beauty and love in life.

Deer people are beautiful both physically and spiritually, as they radiate love and concern for others in all their thoughts, words, and actions. They are attracted to all things beautiful themselves and will often possess works of art and numerous items of colorful clothing. Nature and the great outdoors also attract the attention of gentle Deer people.

Deer people are also skillful with language and use their quick minds and intuition. They possess the gift of gab and appear quite jovial and witty when in the company of others. Many Deer people are often termed "socialites." Deer are energized when around others, far more so than when they are on their own. Given their active type of energy, Deer people like to be kept busy and entertained. Deer people have no interest in changing other people; their focus is on being socially desirable themselves.

ELEMENTAL CLAN

As their birth time element is Air, Deer belong to the Butterfly clan. Butterflies are colorful and graceful. They begin life as caterpillars, only to be transformed into their beautiful and free-flowing state after an intense, cocoon-wrapped metamorphosis. To the Native Americans, they are a symbol of change, transformation, and hope.

Like the butterfly, Deer people are beautiful to behold and delightful to have around. They are active, energetic, and ever changing, in physical appearance as well as in their feelings, thoughts, and opinions. As such, they have the power to transform and uplift those around them. They are intelligent, innovative, and expressive individuals. But their appearance and behavior can be most deceiving, even to themselves. If they are nurtured and respected, they will remain calm and refreshing. If they are angered, they may quickly erupt into an overpowering fury.

SEASONAL ELEMENT

Your seasonal totem animal, the Eagle, is closely related to the element governing the season in which you were born. For more information about your seasonal totem animal and your seasonal element, Fire, see pages 86–87.

- *Strengths to cultivate* Flexibility, *spirituality, optimism, humanitarianism
- *Possible weaknesses to address* Lack of practicality and perseverance, lack of control in emotional responses

DOG ●

YEARS OF BIRTH: 1910, 1922, 1934, 1946, 1958, 1970, 1982, 1994, 2006, 2018

WHO AM I?

NATURAL ENERGY	Yang
NATURAL ELEMENT	Earth
CORRESPONDING TIME	(Dog ascendant) 7 P.M.–9 P.M.
CORRESPONDING MONTH	October
CORRESPONDING DIRECTION	West/northwest
CORRESPONDING SEASON	Late fall (autumn)
CHARACTER TRAITS	Loyal, dutiful, unselfish, honest, idealistic, courageous, trustworthy, tolerant, faithful, responsible, anxious, capable, honorable, kind, generous, compassionate, heroic
PERSONAL NEEDS	Dogs need to be rewarded often and told how much their loyalty and devotion is appreciated by the lucky people in their lives
LIFE CHALLENGES	To love and care for themselves and to learn to ask for what they want

TEMPERAMENT

People born in the year of the Dog are idealistic and highly principled. They have strong beliefs and live by their morals. To a Dog, everything in life is black or white, right or wrong, good or bad—there is no middle ground. Dogs hate injustice, insincerity, and disloyalty.

Dogs are champions of the downtrodden, loyal supporters of just causes, and totally self-sacrificing. They need a purpose in life in order to feel content and will often put the interests of others before their own. Alert, watchful, and perceptive, Dogs are cautious and rely on their instincts to pick just the right time to jump and make their mark.

Dogs do not place too much importance on money or possessions. What really matters to them is the freedom to do and say what they like. They will go their own way in life, untroubled by conventions, and speak out loudly for what they regard as their own rights or those of others. They also love their creature comforts—a warm bed, a favorite chair, or sitting by an open fire in winter.

LOVE AND RELATIONSHIPS

Dogs make thoughtful and loyal lovers who take their time to fall in love. Dog lovers are more affectionate than passionate and can

easily become hurt and depressed by the words and actions of their lovers. Once Dogs commit themselves, they become deeply attached to their partners and can be a little possessive. Dogs' partners will need to reward their faithful Dog lovers with lots of praise and reassurance to relieve them of their general anxiety about the relationship, as well as their jealousy and suspicions.

Dogs are dependable when it comes to their families, and their children will delight in their playful company. They take their family responsibilities seriously and will be devoted and steadfast in their loyalty. They also like taking on the provider role and will put the needs of relatives ahead of their own.

Dogs are friendly and straightforward with friends. As they can be a little suspicious of strangers, they will tend to hold back before making conversation. This strategy can work well for them, as they may be so generous that some less reputable types will take advantage of them.

WORK AND BUSINESS

Dogs take great pride in their work and treat their employers and colleagues as extensions of their family unit. Dogs are the type who will stay committed to one organization for decades. Many Dogs will choose a career in law, where they can address their keen sense of injustice. Other ideal occupations for Dogs include charity worker, missionary, judge, doctor, police officer, or religious leader.

In Chinese astrology, each of the five elements—Metal, Water, Wood, Fire, and Earth—are dominant in a particular year. This imbues the animal associated with each year with a particular character.

- If you were born in 1934 or 1994, you are a **WOOD DOG**.
- If you were born in 1946 or 2006, you are a **FIRE DOG**.
- If you were born in 1958, you are an **EARTH DOG**.
- If you were born in 1970, you are a **METAL DOG**.
- If you were born in 1922 or 1982, you are a **WATER DOG**.

DRAGON ●

YEARS OF BIRTH: 1916, 1928, 1940, 1952, 1964, 1976, 1988, 2000, 2012

WHO AM I?

NATURAL ENERGY	Yang
NATURAL ELEMENT	Earth
CORRESPONDING TIME	(Dragon ascendant) 7 A.M.–9 A.M.
CORRESPONDING MONTH	April
CORRESPONDING DIRECTION	East/southeast
CORRESPONDING SEASON	Late spring
CHARACTER TRAITS	Dynamic, lucky, exciting, idealistic, enthusiastic, confident, vital, extravagant, energetic, physical, powerful, creative, ambitious, adventurous, brave, optimistic, intelligent
PERSONAL NEEDS	As Dragons can sometimes question their own magnificence and obvious talents, they occasionally need to hear sincere appraisals of their competence.
LIFE CHALLENGES	To appreciate commitment, inner calm, and the feelings of others

TEMPERAMENT

As the only mythical creature in Chinese astrology, the Dragon inspires wonder, excitement, and admiration. Dragons are colorful, confident, and vibrant in personality, and win the attention and support of others with great ease. Dragons like to participate actively in life, engaging their hearts and minds fully with everything that seizes their interest. However, they are free spirits, and will move swiftly to anything that seems more enticing. Blessed with good luck, great reserves of energy, and optimism, Dragons are skilled at leading, taking on projects few others would be prepared to undertake.

Dragons are magnetic, intelligent, and extremely self-confident, able to brush aside life's obstacles easily to ensure much personal success. They love to be the focus of attention and at the helm of every project. Their personal charisma has others full of awe and admiration. Dragons are free spirits, sensitive to their environment, and in constant need of new experiences and adventures. They also have fiery tempers.

They are usually very lucky in terms of material wealth. This is just as well, because those born children of the Dragon are much inclined to favor the luxurious and the expensive things in life.

Those born under the influence of the Dragon often have some special connection with water.

LOVE AND RELATIONSHIPS

Outgoing, engaging, and extroverted, Dragons need a lot of friends and social activities to stimulate their excitable natures. Their friends will also need to be upbeat and adventurous or Dragons will soon tire and move on to more attractive acquaintances. They do not need deep or long-term friendships.

Dragon children are good students and quite athletic, preferring to spend their time outdoors; they will enjoy being at school if they are kept motivated. As parents, Dragons will keep their families busy taking regular vacations and hosting many social events. Dragons need to be loved, and relish the adoration of others, particularly those to whom they are attracted. Younger Dragons tend to have a fascination for the new and exciting, leaving them with a short-term

focus. However, as they mature, the idea of commitment becomes more appealing.

WORK AND BUSINESS

Dragons enjoy having a leadership role, thriving as chief executive officers, managing directors, or senior partners. Some career choices include visual artist, photographic journalist, adventurer, athlete, artist, or entrepreneur. Dragons are renowned visionaries who are talented strategists in business.

In Chinese astrology, each of the five elements—Metal, Water, Wood, Fire, and Earth—are dominant in a particular year. This imbues the animal associated with each year with a particular character.

- If you were born in 1964, you are a **WOOD DRAGON**.
- If you were born in 1916 or 1976, you are a **FIRE DRAGON**.
- If you were born in 1928 or 1988, you are an **EARTH DRAGON**.
- If you were born in 1940 or 2000, you are a **METAL DRAGON**.
- If you were born in 1952, you are a **WATER DRAGON**.

EARTH ●

Dominant Element in Chinese Astrology
YEARS OF BIRTH: 1918, 1919, 1928, 1929, 1938, 1939, 1948, 1949, 1958, 1959, 1968, 1969, 1978, 1979, 1988, 1989, 1998, 1999, 2008, 2009

WHO AM I?

1948, 2008 • EARTH RAT

Water controlled by Earth: Stability and direction Earth rats are logical realists who reflect carefully before making any decisions. Full of good advice, Earth Rats rarely make a wrong move and give valuable advice to family, friends, and business associates. They are at peace with and accepting of life's ups and downs.

1949, 2009 • EARTH OX

Double Earth: Practicality and worldly wisdom Earth Oxen are wise, practical, and patient. They can be quite resourceful when it comes to solving problems and often achieve their aims. Being able to engage with their emotions is their main challenge.

1938, 1998 • EARTH TIGER

Earth utilized by Wood: Core strengths are harnessed Earth Tigers have more common sense, patience, and practicality than other tigers. They are stable individuals who value the security of a solid foundation—a job, a home to call their own, and caring friends and family.

1939, 1999 • EARTH RABBIT

Earth utilized by Wood: Core strengths are harnessed
Traditionalist Earth Rabbits tend to be inflexible about ethics, values, and principles. They can be prudish and judgmental. They work hard for their cherished security and do not take risks.

1928, 1988 • EARTH DRAGON

Double Earth: Practicality and worldly wisdom Earth Dragons are more sedate and calm than other Dragons. Their lives are less chaotic, as they are able to recognize and follow wise counsel. They are practical, realistic, and emotionally balanced.

1929, 1989 • EARTH SNAKE

From Fire comes Earth: Powerful and enhancing Earth Snakes are gentle souls with no hidden agendas. They radiate tranquillity and calm. Their genuine care for others is demonstrated in their open communication style. They make good facilitators and counselors.

1918, 1978 • EARTH HORSE

From Fire comes Earth: Powerful and enhancing Earth Horses are able to find the stability and focus often missing in Horses' lives. They are resourceful and will apply their energy to achieving long-term goals. Earth Horses are blessed with a balance of worldly wisdom and youthful exuberance.

1919, 1979 • EARTH SHEEP

Double Earth: Practicality and worldly wisdom Earth Sheep are focused on achieving spiritual fulfillment throughout their lives. They have a strong spiritual side. Earth Sheep are truly caring and compassionate souls, willing to sacrifice much in order to better the lives of others.

1968, 2028 • EARTH MONKEY

From Earth comes Metal: Engaging and activating Earth Monkeys are more interested in lending their mental dexterity to useful pursuits than to fun and games. They are interested in lifelong learning, taking evening classes and acquiring many qualifications.

1969, 2029 • EARTH ROOSTER

From Earth comes Metal: Engaging and activating Earth provides the usually flamboyant Rooster with much needed reserve in both dress and communication style. Earth Roosters do not avoid accountability. They are practical and grounded, full of common sense and responsibility.

1958, 2018 • EARTH DOG

Double Earth: Emphasis on balance and worldly wisdom Earth emphasizes these Dogs' reliability and steadfast devotion, and ensures they do not fall prey to depression and self-doubt. Earth Dogs are therefore more able to take negative blows. They take their commitments seriously. They are realistic and very practical, thriving on methodical and detailed work.

1959, 2019 • EARTH PIG

Water is controlled by Earth: Directed and grounded Earth Pigs make natural homemakers. They desire security and do not value careers, travel, or an adventurous life. Earth Pigs are happiest when married with children and comfortably settled in their family home.

EARTH

In the Native American belief system, Fire, Water, Air and Earth are the four elements considered the most important natural forces. They permeate every aspect of life, ensuring that living things go through a recurring process of birth, life, death, and regeneration. The different elements also cause differences in personality, highlighting particular strengths and weaknesses of character. The elements are also the foundation of many other aspects of the natural world. The following table outlines the correspondences of Earth.

WHO AM I?

KEY ATTRIBUTES	Stability, balance, patience, practicality, realism
AREAS GOVERNED BY THE ELEMENT	The physical body and physical sensations
SEASON OF LIFE IT GOVERNS	Fall (autumn)
DIRECTION	West
TIME OF DAY IT GOVERNS	Afternoon to sunset
TIME OF LIFE IT GOVERNS	Middle life (40–60 years)
ANIMAL BIRTH TOTEM	Beaver: 4/20–5/20 (N); 10/23–11/21 (S) Brown Bear: 8/23–9/22 (N); 2/19–3/20 (S) Snow Goose: 12/22–1/19 (N); 6/21–7/22 (S)
ANIMAL SEASONAL TOTEM	Owl, Raven, Snake

We are all affected by two elements influencing our character and behavior at any one time—the element of the birth time animal totem and the element of the seasonal animal totem. If the two elements and their key attributes are taken into account when analyzing each animal totem's character, a more detailed and accurate description of that totem will be gained.

EARTH AS BIRTH TIME ELEMENT

The instinctive behavior of each birth time animal totem is influenced by the birth time element. It is this element that creates the foundation of each animal totem's basic nature—the essence of who you are. Animal totems with Earth as their birth time element are the Beaver (see pages 58–59), Brown Bear (see pages 60–61) and Snow Goose (see pages 156–157).

These animal totems all have patience and practicality at the core of their nature. They tend to operate by using their common sense, which is well developed. They are realistic and emotionally balanced.

EARTH AS SEASONAL ELEMENT

The seasonal animal totem provides additional gifts and qualities. These qualities relate to the totems' inner senses, spiritual endeavors, and general behavior. The animal totems with Earth as their seasonal element are the Owl, Raven, and Snake. These fall (autumn) animal totems have the force of Earth directing their general behavior. Hence, people born during this time generally act with patience and a great deal of realism. They have balanced and stable natures and are practical.

Raven, Snake, and Owl people all have the capability and wisdom to hold powerful and responsible positions within the community, such as those of the leader, healer, or teacher. They are calm and confident in any situation. They enjoy twilight—late afternoon—a time when they can reflect on and appraise what they have achieved throughout the day. They represent the midlife of human lifetime, from approximately forty to sixty years of age.

The fall (autumn) time animal totem is the Grizzly Bear. Grizzly Bears are enormous and powerful creatures; they lead calm and mostly peaceful lives. They are slow moving, but every move is one of determination and confidence. Their hibernation is believed by Native Americans to demonstrate their obvious capacity for introspection, renewal, and the gaining of wisdom.

PURE SIGNS

Pure signs occur when the season and birth time elements are the same. In animal totem astrology, there are only three animal totems that are pure signs—Air of Air, Fire of Fire, and Water of Water. There is no Earth of Earth.

EIGHT ●

Birth numbers or personal destiny numbers are easy to calculate. Discarding all zeros, total your date, month, and year of birth and reduce that figure to one digit. For example, if you were born on June 27, 1960, number four would be your personal destiny number: 6 + 2 + 7 + 1 + 9 + 6 = 31 = 3 + 1 = 4.

WHO AM I?

GENERAL CHARACTERISTICS	Number Eight is ambitious, tenacious, reliable, honest, and trustworthy
RULING PLANET	Saturn
ELEMENT	Earth
COLORS	Black, purple
GEMSTONES	Amethyst, ruby

TEMPERAMENT

Those with a birth number of eight will typically focus most of their attention on material matters and their careers. They are determined, ambitious individuals with a strong need to excel in their professions. They usually have the strength of will and the tenacity to do so.

While more than happy to achieve positions of power and amass personal wealth, they also have a need to be recognized publicly for their achievements. This may lead them to express their prosperity through their clothing, jewelry, and various status symbols. Despite their somewhat serious natures, Eights do not lack charm, particularly when their projects are flourishing.

Eights generally have a constitution that almost matches their will in terms of strength. At times, however, this can be undermined by their obsession with work. They are reluctant to take time off and often bored on vacation, and many of their medical problems arise from being overworked. While some neglect their bodies as if they were inconveniences, most Eights are level-headed enough to know that a restrained and well-balanced diet and moderate exercise are necessary if they are to function effectively.

They do, however, become annoyed when their bodies begin to flag and may be tempted to abuse stimulants such as caffeine and other substances to keep them on their feet. Other ailments associated with the number eight are tension headaches, glandular problems, rheumatism, and skin and teeth problems.

Eights' native caution makes them unlikely to take on any challenge to which they feel unequal. Consequently, once they have committed themselves to a certain path, their need for success can bring out absolute ruthlessness to claw their way to the top. This callous and uncompromising behavior usually manifests only when failure becomes a real possibility, but when it does, it can lose Eights a great deal of friendship and support.

Often, Eights' instinctive philosophy is to win at all costs. They need to remind themselves periodically that, in reality, such costs are simply too high. Eights must focus on a sense of perspective, avoiding arrogance and ostentation when successful and warding off anger and depression when faced with delays or failure.

LOVE AND RELATIONSHIPS

Since power and achievement are very attractive to certain types of people, Eights often find themselves surrounded by admirers. They are usually perceptive enough, however, to tell when this attraction is purely superficial and so prefer to find friends and partners among those similarly successful in their fields (preferably in different fields, since the competitive nature of an Eight can otherwise cause friction). Their forcefulness and obsession with work will often alienate those not similarly motivated.

The sober, somewhat conventional qualities of Eights make them disinclined to leap into relationships with any spontaneity. Once an attachment has been forged, however, they are extremely loyal and expect to be treated likewise. Since success is so important to them, they can be deeply injured by rejection, infidelity, and deceit.

WORK AND BUSINESS

Accomplishment in this area is the highest priority of Eights. Fortunately, their combination of professionalism, caution, and financial skills gives them a strong basis for achieving their goal. They are very well suited to careers in accounting, banking, investment, and the law (particularly business law). Despite their fondness for personal success, they often enjoy cultivating the skills of others and may consequently be effective in personnel and corporate management. They may also enjoy the challenges of being entrepreneurs or agents.

Eights aspire to a stable, businesslike manner at all times, but may often lose patience with professional ineptitude and those obstructing their progress.

ELEVEN ●

Birth numbers or personal destiny numbers are easy to calculate. Discarding all zeros, total your date, month, and year of birth and reduce that figure to one digit. For example, if you were born on June 27, 1960, number four would be your personal destiny number: 6 + 2 + 7 + 1 + 9 + 6 = 31 = 3 + 1 = 4.

WHO AM I?

GENERAL CHARACTERISTICS	Number Eleven is concerned with spiritual evolvement. People with this number have unusual destinies.
RULING PLANET	Moon
ELEMENT	Water
COLORS	Cream, green
GEMSTONES	Jade, pearl, moonstone

TEMPERAMENT

As one of the master numbers, eleven indicates individuals for whom life has an unusual and influential plan. Eleven can be reduced numerologically to Two, which suggests the path Elevens will take if they fail to realize their full potential. The natural tendency of Twos to maintain harmony is heightened in Elevens so their lives become a demanding quest for enlightenment, for both themselves and others. Psychic, charismatic, and visionary, Elevens frequently attract devotees who are convinced they are following an individual able to bridge the mundane and spiritual worlds. It is Elevens' duty to see that they do not misuse this influence.

While those whose birth number is two have a healthy regard for balance and moderation, Elevens are more likely to proclaim this as a vital principle for humanity, while utterly disregarding it in their own lives. Like missionaries who consider their own health and safety of small importance compared to the message they bear, they will often endanger themselves through self-neglect or exposure to the most hazardous of conditions if they feel this will further their cause. Running primarily on nervous energy, they are prone to exhaustion, hypertension, and even mental illness. It is vital for Elevens to remember that in order to achieve their goals, they must take time out to relax, eat wisely, exercise, and otherwise restore the balance between body and mind.

Elevens are both blessed and cursed by their ability to envision a better world. Their impatience to see their dreams manifested often causes them to be unrealistic, intractable, and temperamental.

Similarly, their intuition may be developed to the point where rational thinking seems cumbersome and unnecessary. This imbalance often loses them much of the support their personal magnetism would otherwise attract. This in turn can lead Elevens to bitterness and pessimism.

Changing the world is naturally a slow and frustrating business, and Elevens who refuse to find a middle ground between the visionary and the practical put both themselves and their ideals at risk. Those who are able to remain partially grounded in everyday life can avoid the potentially self-destructive extremism associated with this number.

LOVE AND RELATIONSHIPS

Elevens share the need of those whose birth number is two to support others, but often this is expressed in terms of all humankind. This worthy, but exacting, ambition often prevents them from achieving genuine intimacy with individuals. They will be patient and encouraging with their friends and partners, but will often find them unable to live up to the extraordinarily high standards they have set for themselves. In these circumstances, Elevens' passionate honesty may override their innate kindness, forcing them to express this disappointment, despite the pain they might cause.

Partners or close friends of Elevens, therefore, require forgiving and pragmatic natures. They also need to be able to accept the fact that, for Elevens, individuals will always play second fiddle to humanity at large.

WORK AND BUSINESS

The rather otherworldly nature of Elevens will often make it exceptionally difficult for them to choose a career. Working purely for material gain or status will seem almost incomprehensible notions to them, so they will need to find fields in which their desire to create global change and spiritual growth will be assets rather than liabilities.

Elevens often find fulfillment in the arts, psychology, or religion. As natural public speakers, they may chose to utilize their talents within traditional religion, alternative spirituality, or secular motivational lecturing. Politics may also attract them.

FIRE ●

Dominant Element in Chinese Astrology
YEARS OF BIRTH: 1916, 1917, 1926, 1927, 1936, 1937, 1946, 1947, 1956, 1957, 1966, 1967, 1976, 1977, 1986, 1987, 1996, 1997, 2006, 2007, 2016, 2017

WHO AM I?

1936, 1996 • FIRE RAT
Fire controlled by Water: Opportunity to control the darker side
Fire Rats are always on the go both physically and mentally, finding it hard to slow or even rest. Fire Rats are more forthright and passionately outspoken than other Rats and do not usually suffer from this sign's tendency toward stress and anxiety.

1937, 1997 • FIRE OX
From Fire comes Earth: Powerfully enhancing This is one Ox you want as a friend and never as an enemy. Fire Oxen have volatile personalities and can pack quite a force both physically and verbally when challenged or confronted. For all their huff and puff, they are also full of enthusiasm and passion.

1926, 1986 • FIRE TIGER
From Wood comes Fire: Passion and energy Fire Tigers exhibit enormous energy and magnetism. They are courageous, taking unthinkable risks. Fire Tigers pack a lot of activity and adventure into their lives and want constant change in their careers and relationships.

1927, 1987 • FIRE RABBIT
From Wood comes Fire: Passion and energy Gusto, courage, and motivation are just what Rabbits require to really get going. Fire Rabbits are the most successful Rabbits in high-profile professions. They are able to blend intuition and reflection with personal magnetism and are often hugely popular individuals.

1916, 1976 • FIRE DRAGON
From Fire comes Earth: Powerfully enhancing Fire Dragons seem like bolts of lightning—magnetic, magnificent, energizing, and awe-inspiring. They are totally aware of their effect on others and take

pleasure in it. Their life is full of dazzling social engagements, interesting people, and exciting places.

1917, 1977 • FIRE SNAKE

Double Fire: Energy and dynamism Double Fire gives these Snakes all the physical resources they require to match their superior intellects. Fire Snakes are unstoppable in business and will achieve high status quickly and with ease.

1966, 2026 • FIRE HORSE

Double Fire: Energy and dynamism Double Fire blows the energy meters off these Horses. They are hurried, daring, and restless. Fire Horses have many projects going at one time and find it hard to concentrate on details or decide on a methodical approach. They will also find commitment difficult and are more comfortable single.

1967 • FIRE SHEEP

From Fire comes Earth: Powerfully enhancing Fire Sheep have the willpower and motivation to achieve their goals. Unlike other Sheep who are more idle and placid, Fire Sheep are confident and have warm, caring, and winning personalities. Fire Sheep make appealing socialites and good networkers.

1956, 2016 • FIRE MONKEY

Metal molded by Fire: Intensity and direction Fire Monkeys are focused on power and control from an early age. This is not a personality given to compassion and a sense of fair play. They can be ruthless and have flexible values and principles if necessary.

1957, 2017 • FIRE ROOSTER

Metal molded by Fire: Intensity and direction Fire Roosters are bold, direct, and blunt. They can appear extremely loud and colorful. Fire Roosters like to make dramatic entrances, parade across grand dance floors, and generally be the focus of attention.

1946, 2006 • FIRE DOG

From Fire comes Earth: Powerful and enhancing Fire Dogs do not lose sight of their own needs and desires as other Dog types do. They are passionate about humanitarian causes and quietly confident of their ability to make a real difference. They require little effort to win others' support and generally lead a comfortable, emotionally fulfilled life.

1947, 2007 • FIRE PIG

Fire controlled by Water: Action Fire Pigs are proactive, confident, and motivated enough to aim for specific goals. They can be too keen to win others' approval, which can lead to danger.

FIRE

In the Native American belief system, Fire, Water, Air, and Earth are the four elements considered the most important natural forces. They permeate every aspect of life, ensuring that living things go through a recurring process of birth, life, death, and regeneration. The different elements also cause differences in personality, highlighting particular strengths and weaknesses of character. The elements are also the foundation of many other aspects of the natural world. The following table outlines the correspondences of Fire.

WHO AM I?

KEY ATTRIBUTES	Energy, passion, decisiveness, illumination, expansion
AREAS GOVERNED BY THE ELEMENT	The spirit, intuition
SEASON OF LIFE IT GOVERNS	Spring
DIRECTION	East
TIME OF DAY IT GOVERNS	Sunrise to morning
TIME OF LIFE IT GOVERNS	Birth and youth (0–18 years)
ANIMAL BIRTH TOTEM	Hawk: 3/21–4/19 (N); 9/23–10/22 (S) Owl: 11/22–12/21 (N); 5/21–6/20 (S) Salmon:7/23–8/22 (N); 1/20–2/18 (S)
ANIMAL SEASONAL TOTEM	Beaver, Deer, Hawk

Two elements influence our character and behavior at any one time—the element of the birth time animal totem and the element of the seasonal animal totem. If the two elements and their key attributes are taken into account when analyzing each animal totem's character, a more detailed and accurate description of that totem will be gained.

FIRE AS BIRTH TIME ELEMENT

The instinctive behavior of each birth time animal totem is influenced by the birth time element. It is this element that creates the foundation of each animal totem's basic nature—the essence of who you are. Animal totems with Fire as their birth time element are the Hawk (see pages 96–97), Owl (see pages 118–119), and Salmon (see pages 140–141). With Fire as their birth time element, these animal totems are passionate and enthusiastic to the very core of their beings. They tend to operate very energetically and decisively. They are entrepreneurs by nature and tend to thrive on change.

FIRE AS SEASONAL ELEMENT

The seasonal animal totem provides additional gifts and qualities. These qualities relate to the totems' inner senses, spiritual endeavors, and general behavior. Animal totems with Fire as their seasonal element are the Beaver, Deer, and Hawk. These spring animal totems have the force of Fire directing their general behavior. People born during this season generally act with great energy, passion, and decisiveness. They have spirited natures and, generally, well-developed intuition.

People born during spring—Hawk people, Beaver people, and Deer people—are filled with youthful vitality and have a natural interest in personal growth and development. They tend to be early risers, as they want to greet the dawn of each new day. This is the time of day they are at their most productive. They represent the human lifetime of childhood and adolescence, from birth to approximately eighteen years.

The springtime animal totem is the Eagle. Eagles are awesome birds of prey, with tremendous strength and vitality, along with the ability to fly extremely high and far in search of prey. This is believed to give them vision and clarity about both the present and the future. Eagles are believed by Native Americans to be messengers for the Creator of the World, bringing enlightenment to the people of the earth.

PURE SIGN

Pure signs occur when the seasonal and birth time elements are the same. The Hawk is the pure Fire sign (Fire of Fire). People of the Hawk totem demonstrate a great capacity for growth and expansion. They are highly energized, extremely passionate and spirited individuals. With such highly developed physical energies, Hawk people are challenged more than any other sign to keep under control the fires that can burn so fiercely inside them. This means tempering their emotional responses and balancing their vital energies. In particular, they need to take their time, considering the likely consequences of their actions and words before diving in.

FIVE

●

Birth numbers or personal destiny numbers are easy to calculate. Discarding all zeros, total your date, month, and year of birth and reduce that figure to one digit. For example, if you were born on June 27, 1960, number four would be your personal destiny number: 6 + 2 + 7 + 1 + 9 + 6 = 31 = 3 + 1 = 4.

WHO AM I?

GENERAL CHARACTERISTICS	Number Five is extroverted, energetic, resourceful, and daring.
RULING PLANET	Mercury
ELEMENT	Air
COLORS	Gray, white
GEMSTONES	Diamond

TEMPERAMENT

People whose birth number is five are usually live wires—extroverted, intrepid, and with huge appetites for experience and adventure. Fives are highly energetic, positive, and convivial people with an insatiable curiosity about all aspects of life. Their restlessness may prevent them from fully developing their interests and talents, but they will consider this a small price to pay for the freedom to follow their whims and fancies.

Although their self-indulgences and impulsiveness often threaten to exhaust their friends' patience, Fives' wit, charm, and magnetism usually win them over. Frivolous, capricious and flighty as they often are, Fives' warmth and enthusiasm are difficult to resist.

The number five is associated with the nervous system. Fives are therefore inclined to hyperactivity, insomnia, and conditions caused by nervous tension, such as poor digestion and ulcers. Some may also suffer from attention deficit disorder. To rebalance these tendencies, Fives will often benefit from various forms of relaxation and sleep therapy, and should avoid stimulants such as caffeine.

Fives rarely need to be encouraged to exercise. However, they may have a tendency to overexercise. While their instinctive desire to burn excess energy is sound, their adventurous natures often incline them to potentially dangerous sports. These interests can benefit their concentration as well as their bodies, but not surprisingly, Fives are often familiar with sports injuries.

While blessed with many childlike virtues, Fives often exhibit the less desirable qualities of children when bored or frustrated, becoming argumentative, sullen, or even violent. With their fundamentally good nature, they are usually remorseful about any such outbursts almost as soon as they have passed, but on occasion, the damage done by their impulsiveness can only be mended slowly.

Fives' love of freedom can also make them undisciplined, erratic, unreliable, and inconsiderate. Their positive ability to see the richness of life's choices can turn to the negative quality of indecision. Their natural daring can turn into foolhardiness, and their optimism into gullibility. Their challenge in life is to accept a little more responsibility and the necessary worldliness of an adult without extinguishing their natural exuberance.

LOVE AND RELATIONSHIPS

Always effervescent company, Fives seldom lack for companionship. However, although perfect as friends or short-term lovers, they typically shy away from the thought of commitment, wary of being tied down or becoming bored with a relationship.

Often, when Fives do attempt more committed relationships, their passion for freedom undermines their best intentions. They are inclined to drift into flirtation or even promiscuity carelessly and with no regard for the pain this might cause their partners. Not being disposed to insecurity, possessiveness, or jealousy, they have little insight into how these emotions can affect others. This is not to say that Fives are incapable of long, stable relationships. If they find partners with personalities as stimulating and mercurial as their own, they will have little trouble sustaining the romance.

WORK AND BUSINESS

Fives can easily slip into boredom, but produce remarkable work when their interest is engaged. In repetitive or unchallenging positions, they can be absolute liabilities, paying little attention to their own tasks, distracting other workers from theirs, and endangering the entire operation.

Since they are also inherently skillful communicators, the most

suitable career choices for Fives are those that combine this natural talent with a rapidly changing and stimulating workload. They are very well suited to work in journalism, public relations, and advertising. Born with a love of adventure, Fives can also excel in more active careers, such as rescue work and firefighting.

FOUR ●

Birth numbers or personal destiny numbers are easy to calculate. Discarding all zeros, total your date, month, and year of birth and reduce that figure to one digit. For example, if you were born on June 27, 1960, number four would be your personal destiny number: $6 + 2 + 7 + 1 + 9 + 6 = 31 = 3 + 1 = 4$.

WHO AM I?

GENERAL CHARACTERISTICS	Number Four is practical, stable, dependable, honest, and trustworthy.
RULING PLANET	Uranus
ELEMENT	Air
COLORS	Blue, gray
GEMSTONES	Sapphire

TEMPERAMENT

Those whose birth number is four are extremely reliable, practical, conscientious, and well-balanced individuals. Just as four-sided shapes are widely used architecturally for their stability and strength, so the personality of the Four acts as a strong, dependable, and fortifying influence on those around them. Fours feel it their duty to build a secure future and provide protection for themselves, their families, and their communities.

Their methods are often traditional, but they are not afraid of innovation once convinced of its potential. They are well-organized and resourceful and at their most effective when following a carefully thought-out plan and a steady routine.

Although they have a strong constitution, Fours are susceptible to muscular strain and nervous tension as a result of their dedication to both work and constructive leisure activities, such as home renovation and gardening. They will benefit from relaxation techniques such as yoga, massage, and meditation.

Other stress-related complaints that may trouble Fours include anemia, constipation, and lung problems. Some Fours are inclined to overindulge in food (to power them through their days) and intoxicants (to help them relax). Fours should therefore ensure that their diets are low in fat, hot spices, and alcohol. Fortunately, they rarely lack self-discipline and have a keen sense of survival, so they have little trouble implementing changes to their diet and exercise regimens once they have become aware of a problem.

The desire for security that inspires many of Fours' achievements can also make them chronic worriers. They are methodical and painstaking by nature, and their fear of making mistakes can often slow their progress to a snail's pace to the irritation of others and themselves. Their unassuming reliability in both their professional and social circles is often overlooked. If they are unappreciated, they are reluctant to express the resentment or hurt this causes them, and consequently run the risk of sinking into pessimism, cynicism, or depression.

Fours' natural reserve can also give them the reputation among more extroverted individuals of being distant and possibly even a little dull. To prevent this, they must occasionally force themselves to come out of their shell and take the occasional risk.

LOVE AND RELATIONSHIPS

Fours' love of stability leads them to place a high value on long-lasting and deep friendships. Never impulsive, they assess their friends carefully before offering commitment, but once a bond has been forged, they consider it unbreakable.

Even their choice of life partners will be governed by their judgment of the relationship's potential, rather than through impulsiveness and romance. Not the most amorous of partners, they are nevertheless extremely thoughtful, very devoted, and totally faithful. Their tendency to be obsessive about security makes them prone to doubts and jealousy if they feel that their love is not fully reciprocated. Though they keep their feelings disguised, they can be devastated by rejection. Fours make ideal partners for others

who prefer a quiet life but can also prove salvation for less stable personalities.

WORK AND BUSINESS

Fours prefer a well-organized work environment but, when necessary, are prepared to roll up their sleeves and create the order for themselves. They can occasionally be a little inflexible in the face of rapid change, preferring a sense of routine in their work. However, if the routine appears to be unproductive, they can be a major influence in having work practices changed for the better.

Their fondness for projects that produce lasting results, their attention to detail, and their orderly approach to work make them well suited to a range of professions, including architecture, engineering, landscaping, accounting, and office administration.

G

GEMINI ●

BIRTH DATES: May 21 to June 21

WHO AM I?

SYMBOL	*The twins*	
	Gemini's dual nature and drive to connect with others	
QUEST	*Communication*	
RULING PLANET	*Mercury*	
	Communication, intellectual ability, decision-making	
RULING ELEMENT	*Air*	
	Intelligence, articulateness, objectivity, idealism	
POLARITY	*Positive*	
	Impulsivity, excitability, communicativeness, sociability	
QUALITY	*Mutable*	
	Adaptability, flexibility, cohesiveness	
COLOR	*Yellow*	
	Expressive of Gemini's generally optimistic, energetic, versatile nature	
FOOD	*Beans, celery, marjoram, peppermint*	
FLOWER	*Lily of the valley, rose*	
HEALING HERB	*Caraway, dill, lavender, parsley*	
	Prone to trying to do too many things at once, Geminis could find dill tea very calming.	
GEMSTONE	*Moonstone*	
	Characteristic of Gemini's generally sensitive, complex, faithful, romantic nature	
SUITABLE GIFTS	Jewelry featuring silver, moonstone, mother of pearl, or aventurine; lavender-scented pillow; or sleeping mask	

TEMPERAMENT

People born under the sign of the twins usually can turn a hand to many different types of work and study, enjoying the variety. Those born toward the beginning of the sign, until May 27 or thereabouts, are likely to be especially lucky in life, being blessed with a very wide-reaching mental capacity and a jovial nature. All Geminis tend to attract more than their fair share of good luck.

Geminis, who are the gifted communicators of the zodiac, have finely developed instincts for communicating with others and do so very effectively and entertainingly. Their quest is for connection with others, achieved through mutual understanding. Blessed with natural talents, they are able to communicate effectively with others on many different wavelengths and subjects. With such versatile and active minds, Geminis can border on genius one day and can be lost the next day in a sea of contrast and paradox—hence the duality of the star-sign symbol.

Those born under the sign of Gemini can be quite ambitious. Often they are also original thinkers. With a new idea to pursue, Geminis are inclined to dash off without waiting to devise a strategy for success. Fortunately, being adaptable and quick-witted, Geminis usually overcome their lack of planning and with their fabled luck, they tend to crash through rather than simply crash.

Some Geminis may get themselves into trouble by engaging in risky—though exciting—pastimes, such as gambling. "Double or nothing" is often their motto. But knowing when to quit, either when ahead or behind, can be a problem for the optimistic and energetic Gemini.

Personal areas that Geminis may need to develop include improving their initiative, tenacity, and focus. Worrying about relatively unimportant matters is another weakness that may need to be addressed.

LOVE AND RELATIONSHIPS

Personally as well as professionally, Geminis tend to do well with partners who are more levelheaded, cautious, and serious than themselves. Such partners complement the Gemini dynamo.

Even though Gemini men and women may be flamboyant to the point of flirtatiousness, they demand unequivocal faithfulness from a partner and will be shattered by infidelity. They like their partners to be home-oriented, even homebodies, though they themselves rarely are. Often, a Gemini person will find peace amid natural surroundings, gravitating to hobbies such as recreational sailing, hiking, or bird-watching, so partnership with another person who enjoys noncompetitive outdoor pursuits is well augured.

On the negative side, Geminis can be irritating, especially when they are tired or frustrated. Their imaginative and impulsive natures may mean they try to do or think about too many things at once, making them quite exhausting companions. Do not expect a restful life if you are, or are close to, a Gemini.

WORK AND BUSINESS

Geminis usually find success easily in their professional lives. They have the gift of gab and innate interpersonal and presentation skills; this assures them of much support and fanfare. Their addiction to reading and self-education means they naturally embody the concept of lifelong learning, and they will be employable up to and well beyond retirement.

Their abundance of optimistic and positive energy may mean that a career in sales, marketing, or public relations will appeal to them, along with more classically creative endeavors such as music and the visual arts. Involvement in design, decorating, or color-

related projects are all favored, as many Geminis have a strong aesthetic sense.

They may also favor work that puts them in contact with many people and gives them a variety of different tasks to do during the course of the day. Geminis do well professionally within the world of print or electronic media. In particular, they seem well suited to photography, journalism, or other work in newspapers, magazines, or television.

It is quite usual for Geminis to have more than one career, sometimes simultaneously. They also may be found working and studying at the same time. Such study may be a hobby, a healthy outlet for excess Gemini energy and ability.

It is also quite usual for Geminis to switch careers in early middle life and chase success in a completely different direction. Again, the luck that seems to travel with those born under this sign seems to protect them from the total disaster that often awaits others who attempt to change course midstream.

Geminis need a constantly changing, even pressurized, work environment to sustain their interest and keep them mentally stimulated. For Geminis, following their instincts and taking chances in business, often in terms of foreign interests, seems to bear fruit more often than not. They need to work with people who can keep them on track and provide instant feedback on their ideas. Left alone or unchallenged, Geminis can become rudderless and unproductive.

A tenacious and patient business partner who revels in detail is a boon to the Gemini. Geminis usually need someone to follow through for them, to supply the practical backup necessary to implement their many bright ideas—the fallout from a typical Gemini brainstorm.

Gemini bosses are approachable and popular. They value open communication in the office and make skilled managers of difficult people. Encouraging and motivating to all, they use their social skills to lower political barriers and build productive teams.

BLENDING THE SYSTEMS

Geminis born in May

May Geminis are gregarious, chatty, versatile, and intelligent, but apt to make bad choices in relationships, as they tend to choose lovers who are not as pleasant as they first seemed. The Chinese Snake sign ensures Geminis keep important secrets to themselves while appearing to be outgoing and friendly. The receptive Fire element gives them a touch of glamour and a love of show business, as well as talent of their own and a desire to be among exciting and talented people. The Native American Deer of the Butterfly clan makes the Gemini an excellent friend who can counsel others without judging them, but who will jump from one idea to another from one moment to the next.

Geminis born in June

June Geminis are excellent communicators who are capable of doing many things at the same time, but they may suffer in relationship matters. The Chinese Horse makes them excellent salespeople, with a love of travel and a need for freedom. This is enhanced by the active Fire nature, which can lead them into a career in the military or a life of travel, change, and adventure. The Native American sign of Deer of the Butterfly clan makes Geminis a tonic for those who are around them, as they are never boring.

H

HAWK

BIRTH DATES: Northern Hemisphere: March 21 to April 19
Southern Hemisphere: September 23 to October 22

WHO AM I?

BIRTH TIME ANIMAL TOTEM	Hawk
BIRTH TIME ELEMENT	Fire
ELEMENTAL CLAN	Thunderbird
ENERGY FLOW	Active
LIFE PATH	To pace oneself in everyday life and reflect more on the likely outcomes of one's actions before taking the initiative
PERSONAL GIFTS	Foresight, energy, optimism, perceptiveness, boldness, honesty, sincerity, independence
PERSONAL CHALLENGES	Rashness, willfulness, impatience, impulsiveness
CORRESPONDING SEASON	Early spring—a time of birth, of new life and budding, and of awakening from winter's hibernation
SEASONAL ELEMENT	Fire
SEASONAL TOTEM	Eagle
COLOR	Yellow
PLANT	Dandelion
GEMSTONE	Opal

HAWK PEOPLE

Native Americans believe that hawks are messengers of the sky. Seeing one or hearing its cry is an omen of new arrivals or new things about to happen, either good or bad. Hence seeing or hearing a hawk signals the need to become more aware of the environment and to be prepared for change.

Hawk people are often seen as the messengers of insight and the seekers of truth, demonstrating keen perceptiveness and foresight in their daily lives as well as in the lives of others. Nothing can quench their determination to uncover the truth in all matters.

Hawks are big-picture people, who need to see the overall plan before they can attend to minute details. However, once they are committed to an overall plan, Hawks can easily apply their acute perception even to minor aspects, ensuring that few, if any, details are left unattended.

Action-oriented, bold, and quick, given their active energy-flow type, Hawks prefer initiating new ideas and projects rather than attending to completion. Once things are up and running, they prefer to lead others, getting them to attend to day-to-day routine activities and completion.

Hawks often fly from one project to another quite quickly, as this suits their lightning-fast minds. As this swift energy comes only in short bursts, long-range projects are best avoided. Hawks readily and quite naturally embrace change.

ELEMENTAL CLAN

As their birth time element is Fire, Hawk people belong to the Thunderbird clan. A Native American myth tells how the thunderbird, the largest and most magnificent of the hawks, fell prey to arrogance, developing an inflated ego. In a burst of Fire from a thunderbolt sent by the Creator, it was raised from the earth to become a spirit. Like the thunderbird, Hawk people are powerful, radiant, and passionate. They have spirited and enthusiastic personalities, and thrive on activity and change. They are charming and witty people who love being the center of attention. Just like Fire, their emotions can vary in the extreme, from warm to blazing.

SEASONAL ELEMENT

Your seasonal totem animal, the Eagle, is closely related to the element governing the season in which you were born. For more information about your seasonal totem animal and your seasonal element, Fire, see pages 86–87.

• **Strengths to cultivate** Intuition, physical stamina, optimism, motivation • **Possible weaknesses to address** Gullibility to flattery, inflated ego, oversensitivity to constructive criticism

HORSE ●

YEARS OF BIRTH: 1906, 1918, 1930, 1942, 1954, 1966, 1978, 1990, 2002, 2014

WHO AM I?

NATURAL ENERGY	Yang
NATURAL ELEMENT	Fire
CORRESPONDING TIME	(Horse ascendant) 11 A.M.–1 P.M.
CORRESPONDING MONTH	June
CORRESPONDING DIRECTION	South
CORRESPONDING SEASON	Summer
CHARACTER TRAITS	Independent, headstrong, hardworking, talkative, energetic, dexterous, sociable, strong, bold, intelligent, confident, brave, opportunistic, ambitious, competitive, youthful
PERSONAL NEEDS	Horses need adoration and much space in their relationships and constant stimulation in their work.
LIFE CHALLENGES	To integrate quiet thought, reflection, focus, and tenacity into their daily lives

TEMPERAMENT

Horses are the restless adventurers of the Chinese zodiac. Energetic and active, they are constantly on the move. Never afraid to speak their minds, Horses rush into conversations and debates, no matter how little they may know about the subject. They tend to take on causes eagerly and impetuously, and their impatience and lack of caution can be challenging.

They like to live independent lives and to be free to roam and explore all areas of life. Horses are afraid of being trapped in any situation and want to live without having to commit themselves long term to any person, object, or goal. They love to socialize and to be the focus of attention, often maintaining their good health and youthful appearance far longer than others do.

LOVE AND RELATIONSHIPS

Horses keep their friends on the move. Aside from physical activity, they are more giving than demanding in their friendships. Horses love company and talking, but will set the pace in all shared activities. Horse friends are cheery and optimistic and will do their best to rouse others from their doldrums.

Horses are the energetic youngsters who refuse to grow up. They bring energy, activity, fun, and encouragement to a family in any role, whether it is as a parent, sibling, partner, or child. Horses leave the family nest early to feed their worldly curiosity and adventurous spirit. It is rare for Horses to settle down early in life. But when they do settle down, they are quite protective of their families and cherish their children's company.

Horses are virile and physically exhausting as lovers. Blessed with youthful vitality and enthusiasm, Horses leap into love affairs with wild abandon. Unfortunately, their attention span does not encourage long-term commitments. Horses are forever restless for

change and variety and have promiscuous lifestyles. Horse affairs are always short, but memorable.

WORK AND BUSINESS

Horses are good with their hands and can work at a furious pace. This suits them in trades where they are appreciated for their productivity. They make great salespeople and customer service providers—they

need frontline, people-oriented positions where they can use their interpersonal skills to the full. Horses are also advised to seek mobile outdoor positions that will challenge them, keeping them on the move and in a variety of environments. Ideal occupations for Horses include photographer, photojournalist, traveling salesperson, technician, tour operator, jockey, or racecar driver. Their manual skills can also earn them a good living, so building, cabinetmaking, or craftwork may suit them.

In Chinese astrology, each of the five elements—Metal, Water, Wood, Fire, and Earth—is dominant in a particular year. This imbues the animal associated with each year with a particular character.

- If you were born in 1945 or 2014, you are a **WOOD HORSE**.
- If you were born in 1966, you are a **FIRE HORSE**.
- If you were born in 1918 or 1978, you are an **EARTH HORSE**.
- If you were born in 1930 or 1990, you are a **METAL HORSE**.
- If you were born in 1942 or 2002, you are a **WATER HORSE**.

LEO

BIRTH DATES: July 23 to August 22

WHO AM I?

SYMBOL	*The lion* Leo's power, passion, and authority	
QUEST	*Visualization*	
RULING PLANET	*The sun* Independence, creative drive, spirit, willpower, vitality	
RULING ELEMENT	*Fire* Enthusiasm, confidence, passion, energy	
POLARITY	*Positive* Impulsivity, excitability, communicativeness, sociability	
QUALITY	*Fixed* Stability, loyalty, endurance	
COLOR	*Orange* Strength, richness, positiveness	
FOOD	*Olives, grapefruit, oranges, pineapples, honey*	
FLOWER	*Delphinium, poppy, marigold*	
HEALING HERB	*Bay, borage, and saffron* Crumbling a bay leaf or two into steaming vegetables or simmering pots is a healthy habit for Leos to acquire.	
GEMSTONE	*Sardonyx* Dignity and kingly instincts	
SUITABLE GIFTS	Jewelry featuring gold, sardonyx, amber, and topaz; yellow or orange round candles; items for the dressing table, such as a hand mirror or a set of brushes	

TEMPERAMENT

Leo is the charismatic and eternally optimistic sign of the zodiac. Leos' sunny-natured, vital, larger-than-life personalities ensure their popularity. They are proud and dignified, and the respect and admiration of others drive their heroic deeds and nurture their self-esteem. Leos' nature is generous, outgoing, humorous, and creative, but their standards can be high, which can make them seem arrogant or dismissive of others.

Leos are usually very clever, imaginative, strong, and resourceful people. Farsighted and efficient, they work methodically toward a

bright future, meeting difficulties with a cheerful and warm
countenance, creating opportunities out of obstacles. Leos have a
generosity of spirit, and this adorns any high-profile calling.
Because they love to explore new territory and experience change,
theirs is usually an interesting and full life. Those born around
August 2 are very fond of anything extraordinary.

Perhaps because they are highly
imaginative, infectiously energetic,
and blessed with unflagging
enthusiasm, Leos usually relate well
to children. One characteristic, which
they share with many children, is a
tendency to be contemptuous of
authority for its own sake. They are
equally dismissive of public opinion
and likely to form independent and
discerning views in which they grant
no mercy to the bogus or undeserving. Young Leos starting out in
the professional world should exercise caution when dealing with
their superiors. In business, cultivating tact and the ability to keep
silent when agreement is unlikely are desirable traits to learn.

Leos generally, especially those born from July 26 to July 28,
should be careful to mind their own business and not interfere in
the affairs of others—no matter how outstanding their managerial
talents. Instead, Leos should channel their excess energies into
public service, charitable works, or social groups, where their
infinite capacities for leadership, responsibility, and management
will be welcomed as committed and positive, rather than rejected as
interfering and presumptuous.

The major Leonine weakness is vanity, which can fool Leos into
believing that they can do everything. Unfortunately, upon realizing
their limitations, Leos will find the blow to their pride a very
painful experience. Personal areas that Leos may need to develop
include learning humility, seeking and taking informed advice, and
asking for help when necessary.

LOVE AND RELATIONSHIPS

In love, Leos are passionate, but they may have a habit of falling for
the wrong type of person; when they find the right person, they are
steadfast and faithful.

People born under the sign of Leo need partners who, though quiet themselves, will not be intimidated by any loud roaring or posturing. They should be able to maintain independent interests and opinions while providing support and sympathy for the busy, demanding, outgoing Leo.

Leos would also do well to temper their magnificent and independent personalities with a touch of humility. Without it, they can all too easily convince themselves and others that they need nobody except their own superior selves—and then wonder why they share no meaningful personal relationships!

WORK AND BUSINESS

At work Leos are energetic and efficient, but they can become irritated when things do not go their way. Naturally confident and charming, Leos go out of their way to achieve recognition and distinction in their chosen professions. They are competitive, testing their strength and endurance against that of others. Leos will often

take up causes and lead charities, playing the hero and devising grand plans for a brighter future.

They are excellent organizers and can handle heavy responsibilities with ease; they are excellent at managing large-scale projects and expenditures. They often shine as entrepreneurs, picking trends before others do and pioneering the way in various fields of endeavor. The printing and newspaper industries are clear favorites with Leos, as are catering, entertainment, public administration, and politics. Leos may also be talent scouts, innovative builders or architects, or experts in new-product development.

In a business relationship, Leo's partner should be the one good at accounting and keeping records, with Leo in the foreground as salesperson or spokesperson for the partnership.

Leos are at home in the global arena. They rise to their rightful leadership position in times of crisis or pressure. They forge ahead courageously, heedless of obstacles. Challenging positions that thrust them up front and into the limelight are ideal. They need interaction with others and plenty of action and control in their daily activities.

Leos are the natural leaders of the zodiac. They have great faith in their ability to inspire and manage others. For the Leo boss, mutual respect is important. Loyal and committed staff will be rewarded with noble deeds and generosity. Leo bosses do have to watch their zealousness and fiery strength, however, as these traits may overwhelm the quieter types and come across as arrogance.

BLENDING THE SYSTEMS

Leos born in July

July Leos are ambitious and long for the good things of life, but they are also generous and kind and have a glorious sense of humor. Their greatest love is reserved for their children. The Chinese sign of the receptive Earth Goat lends an artistic eye and the ability to work very hard, indeed. The Earth element makes for efficiency and a scientific turn of mind and also a love of animals. The Native American sign of the Salmon of the Thunderbird clan lends the ability to get to the heart of any matter. Leos make powerful friends but also powerful enemies, despite their well-meaning and generous nature.

Leos born in August

August Leos are particularly passionate and fiery, exhibiting great generosity, humor, and kindness. They also have a great love for their children and pets. However, they are easily irritated by fools or by those who seek to get in their way. The Chinese sign of the Monkey gives them an inventive mind and great commercial ability, while the active Metal element makes them difficult to persuade or influence. The Native American sign of the Salmon of the Thunderbird clan gives them a slightly regal air—but hides a sensitive nature.

LIBRA ●

BIRTH DATES: September 23 to October 22

WHO AM I?

SYMBOL	The scales Libra's challenge to find a balance between personal desires and the needs of others
QUEST	Balance
RULING PLANET	Venus Relationships, social values, beauty, love, harmony
RULING ELEMENT	Air Intelligence, articulateness, objectivity, idealism
POLARITY	Positive Impulsivity, excitability, communicativeness, sociability
QUALITY	Cardinal Spontaneity, restlessness, the desire for action
COLOR	Indigo Regenerating and helpful in countering fear and frustration
FOOD	Apple, rhubarb, apricot, avocado, licorice
FLOWER	Aster, marigold, sweet violets
HEALING HERB	Dandelion Protection and balance for the heart and mind
GEMSTONE	Opal
SUITABLE GIFTS	Jewelry featuring opals or lapis lazuli, novels by favorite authors, gourmet cookware

TEMPERAMENT

The Libran habit of always considering both sides of every
question is usually matched by an even temper, sound common
sense, and practicality. Librans tend to take their time to acquire
any information they need or to measure situations and people.
They are usually able to detect all that is fake or worthless. In
turn, they are trusted and respected by others who admire their
patient behavior and well-considered opinions. But their abiding
Libran desire to strike the right balance in life can mean
they tend at times to be uncertain individuals, ditherers, or
procrastinators.

Some Librans educate themselves further in their later years
simply because their orderly, alert and inquisitive minds enjoy
stimulus. Their preferred fields of study often tend to be
unorthodox. Herbalism, hypnotism—any subject that allows for
inquiry or debate attracts older Librans.

More than most signs of the zodiac, it is the Libran who will demonstrate strength of will and endurance in the face of adversity. Faced with difficult conditions, the Libran response is to persist. Librans will take pleasure, satisfaction, and encouragement from small achievements in the absence of large ones. Adversity, by and large, only makes Librans more determined, more eager, and more efficient in the long run. For this reason, Librans will tend to do well by following rural pursuits either as a hobby or as an income-earning way of life. Poultry keeping, fine horticulture, and the cultivation of novel or hard-to-grow plants are all activities that may appeal to rural-minded Librans.

Librans' fortitude is mirrored in their physical capacity as well, most of them being blessed with constitutions that can withstand great strain. In physical appearance, the Libran man will often be very handsome, the Libran woman a beauty. This personal attractiveness may be quite notable in those Librans born on October 2 or 3. Those born on these days may also be endowed with the gifts of prophecy and charisma. Such Librans can be devastatingly attractive, talented people who will be in demand in any career that depends on widespread public appeal.

Personal areas that Librans may need to develop include addressing procrastination, accepting confrontation when required and confronting others if needed, and lessening dependence on the approval of others.

LOVE AND RELATIONSHIPS

Librans are best suited to having a protective and loving partner, but they can also enjoy their own company. They tend to have reliable and faithful natures, making them excellent partners both personally and professionally. In fact, Librans rarely experience difficulties in attracting partners. Their ideal partners will share a great many Libran interests in both work and play.

Librans like to share and are very generous by nature. For instance, they are usually very happy to entertain large numbers of people at home. Many Librans are particularly good cooks and hosts, being resourceful and thorough when it comes to organizing functions and considering the needs of guests.

Librans are born friendly; they are not inclined to moodiness and are less likely than other signs to suffer from violent likes or 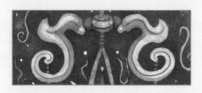 dislikes. They often excel at giving others a shoulder to cry on. Usually quick to grasp the facts of any matter, most Librans are pleased to apply their Libran skills at orderly mental analysis and sound judgment to help their friends. Their talent for friendship often means they enjoy true friends from many walks of life—despite the fact that characteristically warm and easy-going Librans generally are lacking in humor. Strange as it may seem, many Librans have little or no sense of the ridiculous, slapstick comedy, satire, or parody.

WORK AND BUSINESS

Librans, more than other star signs, need to have people around them. They can be found anywhere other than at their desks, preferring to congregate in hallways, tearooms, and open work spaces in order to discuss the latest office happenings. Librans are the supreme networkers of the zodiac. Their charm and ability to handle people makes them excellent agents or arbitrators. They are happiest when among those who encourage them to make the most of their considerable talents.

Given that they are born under the sign of the scales, it is intriguing that quite a number of Librans are interested in work that involves weighing and measuring, in a wide range of  occupations. Librans are often found working as gem merchants, detectives, scientific researchers, scholars, politicians, craftspeople, and producers of finely manufactured goods. One relatively unusual field of endeavor that may well attract Librans is meteorology, in particular, weather forecasting, since this involves balanced analyses of data for formulating predictions. Librans are also attracted to the professions of lawyer, judge, politician, and diplomat.

Librans' ideal environment must be relaxing and harmonious. However, it is not so much the physical environment that counts, as the need to feel accepted and valued by those with whom they work. Hence, for Librans to be happy at work, the culture of the work environment must encourage open communication and the sharing of ideas.

Libran bosses have a people-focused and inclusive management style. They will take the time to get to know and relate to each of their staff members. They will encourage the input and ideas of each individual, no matter how unrealistic. Libran bosses will use their charm to obtain agreement, and are adept at resolving disputes. They can, at times, become opinionated if their gentle manipulations do not produce the desired effect.

BLENDING THE SYSTEMS

Librans born in September

September Librans are noted for their kind hearts and artistic nature. Librans can dither and find it hard to make decisions, but once they have set their mind on something, they usually make a success of it. The Chinese Rooster suggests a wonderful sense of humor and friendliness, but it can also make these Librans opinionated. The receptive Metal element draws them to the world of the arts or the glamour of show business. The Native American Raven of the Butterfly clan ensures they are kind, loving and helpful to others, and their powers of intuition are particularly strong. Being butterflies, they may tend to jump from one idea to the next.

Librans born in October

October Librans have an active mind allied to an artistic nature. The Chinese sign for this month is the active Earth Dog, which gives Librans excellent counseling abilities, but also a naive and trusting nature, which can make them prey to less scrupulous types. The active Earth element adds creativity allied to practicality, which leads to success. Their Native American sign is the Raven of the Butterfly clan, which indicates intuition and a tendency to withdraw when hurt.

METAL ●

Dominant Element in Chinese Astrology
YEARS OF BIRTH: 1900, 1901, 1910, 1911, 1920, 1921, 1930, 1931, 1940, 1941, 1950, 1951, 1960, 1961, 1970, 1971, 1980, 1981, 1990, 1991, 2000, 2001, 2010, 2011

WHO AM I?

1900, 1960 • METAL RAT

From Metal comes Water: Strength and structure Metal gives this Rat mental and physical strength. Metal Rats have strong opinions, and need to voice them often. This can make them appear stubborn and inflexible; however, they balance this with supreme efficiency.

1901, 1961 • METAL OX

From Earth comes Metal: Engaging and activating Metal adds even more physical strength and mental willpower to the Ox. Metal Oxen know exactly what they want and do not waste time. Not usually affectionate by nature, they make up for this by being reliable providers.

1950, 2010 • METAL TIGER

Wood controlled by Metal: Strength and domination Metal Tigers are extremely passionate and volatile, and occasionally overbearing. Loaded with confidence and energy, they are usually quite ambitious and ruthless in business dealings. They demonstrate little of the Tiger's usual easy rapport with others.

1951, 2011 • METAL RABBIT

Wood controlled by Metal: Strength and domination Metal fills a gap, making up for the Rabbit's usual lack of perseverance and bravery. Metal Rabbits are likely to be detached from their emotions when making decisions. They are cunning and manipulative in business affairs.

1940, 2000 • METAL DRAGON

From Earth comes Metal: Engaging and activating The Metal element intensifies the Dragon's magnetic and strong-willed personality. With an abundance of confidence and self-appreciation, Metal Dragons do not easily accept defeat or failure.

1941, 2001 • METAL SNAKE

Metal molded by Fire: Skillful Metal Snakes are too calculating and discriminating for their own good. They want the best life can offer and will set out with cool logic and detachment to find a position of influence and power.

1930, 1990 • METAL HORSE

Metal molded by Fire: Energizing Metal Horses are always on the go. Headstrong and hard to tame, they find it impossible to adapt to routine. Metal Horses are addicted to freedom, open spaces, and constant change. Their boldness and engaging personalities add to their sexual appeal. When focused, they can be quite productive.

1931, 1991 • METAL SHEEP

From Earth comes Metal: Engaging and activating Metal Sheep have stronger characters than other Sheep. They are able to adjust their sensitivities to gain more of what they want from others. Once sure of their foundations, they will embark on a quest for beauty.

1920, 1980 • METAL MONKEY

Double Metal: Intellectual pursuits Double Metal makes these Monkeys intellectually and physically superior to other Monkey types. They rarely rely on others for assistance. They respect money and will rarely take uncalculated risks with it. In social settings, they appear lively, witty, passionate, and convincing.

1921, 1981 • METAL ROOSTER

Double Metal: Intellectual rigor Double Metal makes these Roosters extremely industrious. They are passionate about their careers and demonstrate a flair for investigation, practicality, and detailed decision-making. They can be uncompromising when dealing with others, expecting excellence.

1910, 1970 • METAL DOG

From Earth comes Metal: Engaging and activating Metal Dogs are stern idealists. They are serious individuals, particularly when it comes to questions of morality and justice. They are forthright and like to speak their minds. Metal Dogs often devote themselves to worthy causes.

1911, 1971 • METAL PIG

From Metal comes Water: Strength and structure Metal Pigs have big appetites for all the pleasures in life. Unlike other Pigs, they work hard to acquire their wants. Extroverted, affectionate, and openly demonstrative, Metal Pigs are sexually appealing and can successfully balance work, fun, and love.

MONKEY

YEARS OF BIRTH: 1920, 1932, 1944, 1956, 1968, 1980, 1992, 2004, 2016

WHO AM I?

NATURAL ENERGY	Yang
NATURAL ELEMENT	Metal
CORRESPONDING TIME	(Monkey ascendant) 3 P.M.–5 P.M.
CORRESPONDING MONTH	August
CORRESPONDING DIRECTION	West/southwest
CORRESPONDING SEASON	Early fall (autumn)
CHARACTER TRAITS	Intelligent, witty, entertaining, inquisitive, energetic, optimistic, sexual, competitive, lively, inventive, sociable, talkative, enthusiastic, generous, versatile, restless
PERSONAL NEEDS	Monkeys need constant variety and mental stimulation. They need to be shown appreciation for their wit and charm
LIFE CHALLENGES	To develop self-discipline for their projects and self-control in their relationships

TEMPERAMENT

Monkeys are renowned for their keen intellects and lively, comic personalities. No challenge is too great for these motivated, ingenious intellectuals. Monkeys detest routine and get bored easily with the status quo. They like to test the boundaries in every possible situation. They like change and taking risks. Their principle is to break the rules, live for the moment, and above all, have fun. Their excitement, optimism, and daredevil approach to life are irrepressible, and they make a distinct impression on everyone they meet. Monkeys are also renowned tricksters and teasers, the clever and active clowns of the Chinese zodiac, who search for fun and excitement in everything they do. They are irrepressible eccentrics and highly intelligent.

LOVE AND RELATIONSHIPS

Monkeys are extroverts and will want to socialize frequently with their friends. This can take up a lot of time, as Monkeys love acquiring new friends and are constantly meeting up with different types of people from all walks of life. Monkeys hate being on their own for too long.

Monkeys will only commit to family life or a relationship when they are assured they can still have a fun, socially active lifestyle.

Few Monkeys do well when bogged down with routine, convention, and family chores. Their homes are full of activity, littered by toys, games, and books. Relatives and other visitors are always welcome and cherished for the variety they bring. As children, Monkeys are quite mischievous and will need a good role model to direct their mental dexterity toward worthwhile pursuits.

Monkeys make fun and lively lovers. Morals in the bedroom are not their strong suit. Anything goes for Monkeys—provided it interests them. As they love a challenge, Monkeys are not above competing for the affections of those they desire. Variety and quantity are the key to a happy love life for Monkeys.

WORK AND BUSINESS

Monkeys are gamblers, renowned for being in volatile financial circumstances. Yet, no matter how much they lose, Monkeys never seem to lose their passion for risk-taking. As such, they are great as entrepreneurs. At their best, Monkeys are exceptional planners and organizers who need lots of variety and challenge to keep them motivated and their highly active minds engaged. In the workplace, Monkeys hate routine and hard work, and have short attention spans. They are not the easiest or the most pleasant to work with, but are sure to add brightness to any dull office environment. They are likely to have up-and-down careers, with a lot of erratic job changes. Ideal career choices for a Monkey include comedian, entertainer, actor, traveler, photographer, or social columnist.

In Chinese astrology, each of the five elements—Metal, Water, Wood, Fire, and Earth—are dominant in a particular year. This imbues the animal associated with each year with a particular character.

- If you were born in 1944 or 2004, you are a **WOOD MONKEY**.
- If you were born in 1956 or 2016, you are a **FIRE MONKEY**.
- If you were born in 1968, you are an **EARTH MONKEY**.
- If you were born in 1920 or 1980, you are a **METAL MONKEY**.
- If you were born in 1932 or 1992, you are a **WATER MONKEY**.

NINE ●

Birth numbers or personal destiny numbers are easy to calculate. Discarding all zeros, total your date, month, and year of birth and reduce that figure to one digit. For example, if you were born on June 27, 1960, number four would be your personal destiny number: 6 + 2 + 7 + 1 + 9 + 6 = 31 = 3 + 1 = 4.

WHO AM I?

GENERAL CHARACTERISTICS	Number Nine is humanitarian, creative, psychic, and sensual, and has healing abilities
RULING PLANET	Mars
ELEMENT	Fire
COLORS	Red
GEMSTONES	Bloodstone

TEMPERAMENT

Nines are often driven by a passion to right the wrongs of the world and to initiate social reform. They have a powerful faith in the possibility of beneficial change, deep compassion for the suffering of others, and an absolute loathing for all forms of injustice. Their emotions frequently override their better judgment, and they often appear unrealistic in the eyes of others. This, however, usually reflects the shortsightedness of their critics rather than the impracticality of Nines.

With their minds fixed on global change, Nines are frequently inclined to neglect their own health, particularly their diet. However, once a medical problem attracts their attention, they are likely to apply their acute critical faculties to the problem, researching possible therapies thoroughly and getting a wide range of diagnoses before deciding upon a course of action. Ailments traditionally associated with this number include injuries involving blood loss, kidney disorders, and infections and other problems in the urinary and reproductive systems.

Nines may also develop neuroses when working under excessive pressure, and so should ensure they use both mental relaxation techniques, such as meditation, and exercise to relieve stress.

Nines' commitment to improving the planet inclines them to be overly judgmental of others, treating their minor bad habits as if they were crimes against humanity. At the same time, Nines may be blind to their own faults, their compulsive criticism included. Occasionally mistaking their soapbox for a pedestal, Nines can strike others as being self-righteous, superior, and generally a little too fond of the sound of their own voice. When in this mood, they are not difficult to manipulate through flattery—a weakness of which their opponents are quick to take advantage. Since some Nines have something of a martyrdom complex, this may put them at considerable risk. To avoid such pitfalls, Nines should do their best to retain their sense of perspective and humor at all times.

LOVE AND RELATIONSHIPS

Nines are naturally very open-hearted but can only form very close attachments with those with a similar ideological or spiritual outlook. Differences of opinion on philosophical, political, or religious matters can often cloud relationships. In the absence of such disagreements, Nines are extremely sociable people whose enthusiasm and charm inspire admiration and affection.

Warm, sensual, and often flirtatious, Nines may have phases of promiscuity in their lives. However, their innate sense of fairness and justice makes them uncomfortable with the idea of deceiving a partner once they have formed a relationship. Nines' intensely romantic disposition may cause  problems at times. They are easily hurt by chance remarks or imagined slights, can become possessive, and are often reluctant to allow an unsuccessful relationship to end gracefully.

WORK AND BUSINESS

There is no point at all in Nines attempting to find job satisfaction in any field that is not concerned with social or global betterment. Their ideal careers are in areas such as education, politics, law, humanitarian organizations, and animal welfare.

Nines with strong religious or spiritual beliefs will often become prominent in their fields as speakers, teachers, or missionaries. Though they are generally effective when working within groups, Nines may sometimes alienate others by being overly critical of others' behavior and achievements.

O

ONE ●

Birth numbers or personal destiny numbers are easy to calculate. Discarding all zeros, total your date, month, and year of birth and reduce that figure to one digit. For example, if you were born on June 27, 1960, number four would be your personal destiny number: 6 + 2 + 7 + 1 + 9 + 6 = 31 = 3 + 1 = 4.

WHO AM I?

GENERAL CHARACTERISTICS	Number One is independent and has organizational and leadership abilities.
RULING PLANET	Sun
ELEMENT	Fire
COLORS	Gold, orange, yellow
GEMSTONES	Amber, topaz

TEMPERAMENT

People whose birth number is one are usually brimming with innovative ideas and ambitious goals. They rarely have any interest in treading well-worn ground, preferring to launch themselves into uncharted territory with a genuinely pioneering spirit.

Ones often enjoy expressing their intense sense of individuality through their dress, manner, and lifestyle. They are extremely independent and self-motivated, but will usually admit to enjoying a little praise now and then. Although their determination and drive can make them effective leaders, they are often too preoccupied to give their supporters encouragement in return or even to check whether they are able to keep up.

Ones' preoccupations with their ideas and projects often make them neglectful of their health. Potential areas of trouble for Ones are the eyes, the back, and especially the cardiovascular system. The liver may also cause problems if a balanced diet is not maintained. Ones need to be conscious of their weight and cholesterol levels and should choose exercises such as yoga, swimming, and walking, which have a beneficial effect on the circulation, as well as weight. Impatient with time spent on such maintenance, Ones should be careful not to exercise too strenuously or too quickly.

Many of Ones' problems come from paying much more attention to their internal worlds than to the world and the people outside. Ones' endeavors are sometimes undermined by their tendency to rush through one project to get to the next or by a reluctance to start things because of a fear of failure. As they care so much about their undertakings, their spirits are very vulnerable to disappointment, and a complete disaster can leave them feeling deeply dejected for months—or even years—afterward. The happiest Ones are those who make a point of voluntarily emerging from their private worlds now and then.

LOVE AND RELATIONSHIPS

Because of the rush of ideas constantly filling their heads, Ones often seem emotionally distant to others. Their ideal friends and partners are those who understand this and put an effort into drawing them out of themselves once in a while, while still allowing them plenty of space to explore their thoughts.

In the absence of suitable partners, Ones may feel isolated and  abandoned despite the fact that they are well liked. Their love of independence means that their best choices for romantic partners are either others who are similarly self-contained or those who are devoted and patient enough to live with their erratic attentions. In either case, though, Ones need to make a concerted effort to put their projects aside periodically and give their partners the love and support they deserve.

WORK AND BUSINESS

Natural groundbreakers, Ones need careers that allow them to focus on their goals without interference. They are uncomfortable when their professional duties cast them as team players but thrive as leaders and innovators. These skills make them well qualified for positions in the political arena and the upper echelons of the corporate world. Although they are goal oriented, their ambitions are not necessarily tied to financial gain. Rather, they are concerned with achievement in itself. This non-mercenary approach to work means that Ones are also suited to all fields of exploration, from scientific research to actually leading expeditions into seldom-traveled parts of the world. Their passion and creativity enable many Ones to achieve great success in the arts.

OTTER

BIRTH DATES: Northern Hemisphere: January 20 to February 18
Southern Hemisphere: July 23 to August 22

WHO AM I?

BIRTH TIME ANIMAL TOTEM	Otter
BIRTH TIME ELEMENT	Air
ELEMENTAL CLAN	Butterfly
ENERGY FLOW	Active
LIFE PATH	To develop latent psychic powers consciously, maintain an easy flow of emotion, and regularly touch base with the physical world
PERSONAL GIFTS	Imaginativeness, humanitarianism, youthfulness, perceptiveness, curiosity, empathy, passion
PERSONAL CHALLENGES	Sensitivity, idealism, impracticality, intensity
CORRESPONDING SEASON	The heart of winter—a time of cleansing, purification, and reflection
SEASONAL ELEMENT	Air
SEASONAL TOTEM	White Buffalo
COLOR	Silver/gray
PLANT	Aspen tree
GEMSTONE	Silver

OTTER PEOPLE

Native Americans view the otter as one of the most playful and friendly animals in the wild. Otters appear to live their lives in true bliss. Relaxing and sunning themselves one moment, the next they are quickly attending to the chores of hunting and eating before moving on to playing and cooling themselves in water.

Like their animal totem, Otter people are clever and gentle and have keen intellects, as well as a playful, inquisitive approach to life and a sociable nature. Like their metal and color affinity, silver, Otter people are shiny, flexible, and beautiful to behold. They are viewed as precious additions to a family and community due to their dynamism and their ability to attract good fortune and abundance.

Otter people possess strong powers of perception, intuition, and vision. They display true affection for others, with flowing emotional energy that can make them passionate and ardent lovers. Otter people often have psychic abilities, with a knack for accurately predicting the future.

Otter people make good friends and lively companions, and lift the mood and outlook of everyone around them. Rarely judgmental, Otter people are open-minded, empathetic, tolerant, lighthearted, and generous, and follow the call to humanitarian causes.

Otter people adapt easily to new people and surroundings, and prefer a lively pace. They are independent, individualistic, and true extroverts, which is reflected in their active energy type. They need only rare moments of solitude in order to touch base effectively with their feelings and spirituality.

ELEMENTAL CLAN

As their birth time element is air, Otters belong to the Butterfly clan. Butterflies are colorful and graceful. They begin life as caterpillars, only to be transformed into their beautiful and free-flowing state after an intense, cocoon-wrapped metamorphosis. To Native Americans, they are a symbol of change, transformation, and hope.

Like the butterfly, Otter people are beautiful and delightful to have around. They are active, energetic, and ever-changing, in physical appearance as well as in their feelings, thoughts, and opinions. As such, they have the power to transform and uplift those around them. They are intelligent, innovative, and expressive individuals. But their appearance and behavior can be most deceiving, even to themselves. If they are nurtured and respected, they will remain calm and refreshing. If they are angered, they may erupt quickly into an overpowering fury.

SEASONAL ELEMENT

Your seasonal totem animal, the White Buffalo, is closely related to the element governing the season in which you were born. For more information about your seasonal totem animal and your seasonal element, Air, see pages 48–49.

- *Strengths to cultivate* Flexibility, spirituality, optimism, humanitarianism
- *Possible weaknesses to address* Lack of practicality and perseverance, a lack of control in emotional responses

OWL

BIRTH DATES: Northern Hemisphere: November 22 to December 21
Southern Hemisphere: May 21 to June 20

WHO AM I?

BIRTH TIME ANIMAL TOTEM	Owl
BIRTH TIME ELEMENT	Fire
ELEMENTAL CLAN	Thunderbird
ENERGY FLOW	Active
LIFE PATH	To cultivate and practice tolerance in everyday dealings with others, especially those less gifted and developed
PERSONAL GIFTS	Self-reliance, expressiveness, inquisitiveness, wisdom, justice, sense, intelligence, discretion
PERSONAL CHALLENGES	Conventionalism, intolerance, pride, dominance
CORRESPONDING SEASON	Late autumn—a time of long nights and the arrival of the first snows
SEASONAL ELEMENT	Earth
SEASONAL TOTEM	Grizzly Bear
COLOR	Black
PLANT	Black spruce pine
GEMSTONE	Obsidian (volcanic glass)

OWL PEOPLE

The owl is frequently referred to by Native Americans as the "night eagle" or the "night's friend." A large bird of prey with a distinctive cry, it has huge eyes that give it the power to see through the darkest of nights. Native Americans believe the owl sees and knows everything. Sighting one in the wild is a sign either that you should become more observant of what cannot be seen at a physical level, or that it is time for you to face your darkest fears.

Owl people are intelligent, very observant, and sensible. While young Owls are growing up, they may be described as "wise beyond their years," and wisdom is a gift they carry throughout their lives. Owl people have an inner strength, an ability to be both soft and strong in their personalities

Given their eye for detail and their almost clairvoyant ability to read the thoughts and intentions of others, Owl people are very difficult to deceive. They can get to the heart of any matter in record time, leaving others still confused about how they did it and frustrated in any plan to put one over the wise, all-knowing Owl.

The only risks Owl people take in life are those they have calculated thoroughly. Hence, they rarely make a poor decision or take an incorrect action. Regret is an emotion Owls do not get to experience.

It is not surprising then that in modern society, judges or school principals are often represented as Owls. Owl people have strong ethics and principles and a clear sense of fairness and justice. In addition, they like to be in positions of power—ideally those that will allow them to make decisions about right or wrong, guilt or innocence; they like also to dispense any punishment due.

ELEMENTAL CLAN

As their birth time element is Fire, Owl people belong to the Thunderbird clan. A Native American myth tells how the thunderbird, the largest and most magnificent of the hawks, fell prey to arrogance, and developed an inflated ego. In a burst of fire from a thunderbolt sent by the Creator, it was raised from the earth to become a spirit.

Like the thunderbird, Owl people are powerful, radiant, and passionate. They are spirited and enthusiastic, and thrive on activity and change. They are charming and witty people who love being the center of attention, delighting in acknowledgment and praise from others. Just like fire, their emotions can vary in the extreme, from warm to blazing.

SEASONAL ELEMENT

Your seasonal totem animal, the Grizzly Bear, is closely related to the element governing the season in which you were born. For more information about your seasonal totem animal and your seasonal element, Earth, see pages 78–79.

• *Strengths to cultivate* Intuition, physical stamina, optimism, motivation • *Possible weaknesses to address* Gullibility to flattery, inflated ego, oversensitivity to constructive criticism

OX ●

YEARS OF BIRTH: 1913, 1925, 1937, 1949, 1961, 1973, 1985, 1997, 2009

WHO AM I?

NATURAL ENERGY	Yin
NATURAL ELEMENT	Earth
CORRESPONDING TIME	(Ox ascendant) 1 A.M.–3 A.M.
CORRESPONDING MONTH	January
CORRESPONDING DIRECTION	North/northeast
CORRESPONDING SEASON	Late winter
CHARACTER TRAITS	Reliable, patient, purposeful, conscientious, kind, determined, persevering, hardworking, sensuous, painstaking, dependable, stable, skillful, dexterous, confident, authoritative
PERSONAL NEEDS	Oxen need to be appreciated for their hard work and dependability
LIFE CHALLENGES	To feel more comfortable with their feelings and to be more expressive emotionally

TEMPERAMENT

Oxen are direct, principled, dedicated people who like to tread the well-worn paths of tradition and respectability. They are trustworthy and grounded. Oxen are the most physically powerful and sure-footed animals of the Chinese zodiac—no other sign can match them for physical endurance, tenacity, and patience. Apart from their physical strength, Oxen are also endowed with a keen appreciation of beauty. They will often give in to their need to indulge their senses. Upfront, honest, and practical, Oxen have clear values and beliefs and expect others to operate in the same way. Most of the time they are placid, slow to anger, and quick to forgive.

LOVE AND RELATIONSHIPS

As friends, Oxen are considerate and jovial. They like to spend their rare leisure moments with a small group of trusted friends, indulging in food and wine and appreciating the arts. They are skilled chefs and love giving dinner parties. Oxen are valued for their easy company and practical advice.

Oxen make very grounded, practical, dependable family members. They truly appreciate their homes and families. They want the very best for and from their family members, which can make them quite demanding. They work day and night to ensure the family's financial security, but may not be as attentive to emotional needs. Oxen make very reliable, stable, responsible children, siblings, and parents.

The Ox is not a passionate or romantic sign. As they focus more on work than love, Oxen are not likely to experience numerous sexually charged relationships. They do have an eye for beauty, however, can be quite sensuous, and have great stamina in bed. Not overly demonstrative in public, they will show how much they care by staying monogamous and providing security for their loved ones.

WORK AND BUSINESS

Extremely competent and capable individuals, Oxen shine in the work arena and can remain calm under pressure. Trustworthy and respected for their methodical and detailed approach to projects, they are often viewed as generous and dependable, particularly by colleagues and superiors. They tend to set high expectations for themselves and others, yet they are generous with their time and assistance. Ideal career choices for Oxen include judge, police officer, statistician, administrator, ambulance driver, or government worker.

In Chinese astrology, each of the five elements—Metal, Water, Wood, Fire, and Earth—are dominant in a particular year. This imbues the animal associated with each year with a particular character.

- If you were born in 1925 or 1985, you are a **WOOD OX**.
- If you were born in 1937 or 1997, you are a **FIRE OX**.
- If you were born in 1949 or 2009, you are an **EARTH OX**.
- If you were born in 1961, you are a **METAL OX**.
- If you were born in 1913 or 1973, you are a **WATER OX**.

PIG

YEARS OF BIRTH: 1923, 1935, 1947, 1959, 1971, 1983, 1995, 2007, 2019

WHO AM I?

NATURAL ENERGY	Yin
NATURAL ELEMENT	Water
CORRESPONDING TIME	(Pig ascendant) 9 P.M.–11 P.M.
CORRESPONDING MONTH	November
CORRESPONDING DIRECTION	North/Northwest
CORRESPONDING SEASON	Early winter
CHARACTER TRAITS	Sensual, eager, caring, indulgent, pleasure seeking, fun, lighthearted, optimistic, warmhearted, peaceful, flexible, understanding, generous, happy, shy, modest, sentimental
PERSONAL NEEDS	Pigs need to be supported financially and emotionally and appreciated for the love and sincerity they bring to a relationship.
LIFE CHALLENGES	To set specific goals in life and apply sufficient energy to ensure these goals are accomplished

TEMPERAMENT

Pigs are calm and contented. Stress-free and peace-loving, they are the easiest people to get along with. They like to take life as it comes, focusing on the moment and indulging in everything that delights them. They tend not to set too many goals for themselves, and apply effort only if it will reduce their daily chores instead of increasing them. Calm, friendly, and fun to be with, Pigs are undemanding. However, they do like an opulent life and would prefer this to be provided by someone else. They know how to enjoy life to the fullest, and happiness is their most constant emotional state.

LOVE AND RELATIONSHIPS

Pigs are the easiest people to get along with in the Chinese zodiac. Their generosity, sincerity, and easy-going natures ensure they are often sought for their advice, support, and warm company. As they love to indulge in sensual delights, wining, dining, and dancing all play an important part in a Pig's cherished lifestyle.

Pigs are not attracted to adventure and distant places. They are natural parents and homemakers and show considerable patience and understanding with their loved ones. Pigs are in their element when surrounded by a close family. They are true nurturers. As parents, they want their own children to be achievers, so they can be a little strict to ensure their offspring grow up disciplined—a trait they lack themselves.

Pigs are addicted to love and the art of lovemaking. This sign knows how to engage all the senses in wild abandon, with no care for the consequences. Pigs' lovemaking is enduring, tender, and compassionate. They are openly demonstrative with their partners and will beam in the glow of returned affections. As Pigs are considerate and understanding, they are able to forgive their partners' many trespasses before finally letting go.

WORK AND BUSINESS

Pigs are not usually career- or even work-oriented. They are happy for someone else to be the provider so they can be left at home to nurture. If they must work, they are not too choosy about the occupation—provided the pay is sufficient to meet their needs. Their friendly, easy-going natures ensure their popularity in the workplace. They make enthusiastic team members. Always eager to please, Pigs take their individual responsibilities quite seriously.

In Chinese astrology, each of the five elements—Metal, Water, Wood, Fire, and Earth—is dominant in a particular year. This imbues the animal associated with each year with a particular character.

- If you were born in 1935 or 1995, you are a **WOOD PIG**.
- If you were born in 1947 or 2007, you are a **FIRE PIG**.
- If you were born in 1959 or 2019, you are an **EARTH PIG**.
- If you were born in 1971, you are a **METAL PIG**.
- If you were born in 1923 or 1983, you are a **WATER PIG**.

PISCES

BIRTH DATES: February 21 to March 20

WHO AM I?

SYMBOL	*The fish* Pisceans need to balance their inner emotions with their external reality.
QUEST	*Sensitivity*
RULING PLANET	*Neptune* Psychic powers, escapism, mysticism, sacrifice, uncertainty
RULING ELEMENT	*Water* Psychic powers, escapism, mysticism, sacrifice, uncertainty
POLARITY	*Negative* Receptivity, sensitivity, reserve, the desire for privacy
QUALITY	*Mutable* Adaptability, flexibility, cohesiveness
COLOR	*Aquamarine* Symbolizing luck and alleviating feelings of fear or confusion
FOOD	*Eggplant, spinach, allspice, figs*
FLOWER	*Violet, daffodil, orange blossom*
HEALING HERB	*Lungwort, rose hip*
GEMSTONE	*Aquamarine* Symbolizes elegance, worn for protection when traveling over water
SUITABLE GIFTS	Jewelry featuring aquamarine or amethyst, a new deck of Tarot cards, a romantic dinner for two

TEMPERAMENT

Pisces is a sign concerned with the emotions, creativity, and the psychic world. Imagination and spirituality come naturally to dreamy Pisceans. They have quiet, peaceful, romantic natures, as well as exceptional intuition and an active sixth sense. They are emotional sponges and may sometimes live in an inner world of turbulent feelings. They value their accurate perception of others' feelings and moods, and adjust easily to changing emotional currents.

Rather like their namesake, the fish, Pisceans are seemingly contradictory in many ways. They may appear to have two sides to their personality—they can be kind, caring, and apt to sacrifice themselves for others, as well as surprisingly bossy. However, as Pisceans have a sensitive nature, they are quick to understand the feelings of others.

Pisceans born on February 29 in a leap year are usually very special people who combine the typically Piscean intelligence and capacity for hard work with a most unusual flair for living. The leap day is the birthday of geniuses and highly individual thinkers, the person who is not easily swayed by other people or circumstances and who is never likely to be roped into doing anything he or she does not want to do. Pisceans born on March 5 can often rise to quite prominent heights in politics or industry. As with all Pisceans, they would do well to cultivate the tact and diplomacy necessary at the highest level in both of these fields of endeavor.

Although Pisceans have a basically placid and self-contained nature, they can also be aggressive. This tendency to lash out suddenly is the personal challenge many a Piscean needs to overcome. In many instances, this aggression is prompted by Pisceans' sense of territoriality and their need to assert their presence and authority within their domain. In some it is Pisceans' characteristic self-absorption that limits their consideration for and tolerance of the rights of others who cross their path in life.

The baited hooks of personal power and material success are unlikely to have any attraction for the Piscean. They are quite unimpressed by glamour and have no desire to possess luxurious belongings or enjoy a millionaire's lifestyle.

Pisceans are generous with others, rarely missing a chance to do a good turn. Medieval soothsayers used to counsel Pisceans, above all the other signs in the zodiac, always to help others and to turn a bad deed into a favor. The logic underlying this advice was that, as fish living in a pond are part of a community in which individuals rely for survival on a common code of mutual respect and civilized interaction, so the greatest Piscean good fortune returns as a result of doing favors for others.

Personal areas that Pisceans may consider developing include establishing personal boundaries, setting goals and sticking with them until achieved, and increasing initiative.

LOVE AND RELATIONSHIPS

Pisceans can often be quite suspicious of other people. However, once a friendship has been established, it is likely to be lifelong and very deep. Plenty of tolerance, cheerfulness, and stability on the part of the partner will offset any temperamental Piscean whims or outbursts.

If their partners are creative and imaginative, even poetic by inclination, so much the better, for Pisceans are great romantics. Artistic or otherwise creative people are also more likely to understand the paradoxical Pisceans, in turn tranquil and hyperactive, gentle and aggressive, introverted and extroverted, self-centered and yet affectionate and generous.

Pisceans' partners must also understand their need to pursue their interests, as well as their need to leave the house for days at a time when work calls.

WORK AND BUSINESS

Pisceans are versatile, adaptable, and quick to acclimatize to the organizational culture. Their ability to listen, empathize, and build rapport ensures they are well liked and accepted throughout the organization. They find it easy to make friends with their colleagues and enjoy the social aspects of working with others.

Pisceans are generally diligent people who enjoy applying

themselves quietly to any sort of work where thoroughness, accuracy, a fine eye for detail, reliability, good planning, and organizational skills count. Sometimes Pisceans gravitate toward a business opportunity that involves integrating art into the commodities of

everyday life. They find happiness in graphic design, fashion or furniture design, interior decorating, or architecture. They might choose to put to advantage their ability to process a great deal of detailed information in many fields, such as horticulture, cartography, or publishing.

Pisceans have a great love of learning and often demonstrate a quite remarkable capacity for storing and using knowledge. Librarianship is an obvious career choice, but in more commercial enterprises, it is the Piscean who can take on far more specialized work than, say, the Arian, who is more inclined to entrepreneurial activities.

Pisceans require a fluid, nonrestrictive environment in order to free their self-expression. Aesthetically pleasing surroundings such as museums, galleries, and theaters are ideal for them. They value the opportunity to self-direct their daily tasks and priorities. Their

profound personal integrity and social consciousness are fully
utilized when they are helping others one on one.

Pisceans are rarely drawn to leadership roles—management is
not something they usually aspire to. However, they do make gentle

 and compassionate managers who value
freedom of speech among their staff and
contributions from individuals. Piscean bosses
are skilled at building cohesive teams that
appreciate the space and consideration given
to them.

BLENDING THE SYSTEMS

Pisces born in February

February Pisceans love going out and meeting interesting people,
although they may have trouble telling which hard-luck stories
are true and can waste years rescuing others or fulfilling others'
needs while neglecting their own. However, the Chinese Tiger
gives them a sufficient touch of rebellion and ambition to save
them from being subservient. The active Wood element adds to
their idealism, making them trustworthy, as well as astute and
realistic. Native Americans see the Piscean as a Cougar of the
Frog clan, which gives them a mystical spirit and healing abilities.
They can shut their feelings away when they are hurt and there is
a touch of loneliness about them, but this may actually be an aid
to their clairvoyant abilities.

Pisces born in March

The Water sign of Pisces signifies that the values of a March
Piscean are more spiritual than material. Pisceans, both artistic
and creative, can live a somewhat chaotic lifestyle. The Chinese
sign of the receptive Wood Rabbit implies obstinacy and more of
a temper than a February Piscean has, but it also makes Pisceans
refined and tasteful and gives them a talent for counseling
others. The Native American sign of the Cougar ensures they
are entirely comfortable with the spiritual world, but it can make
it difficult for them to express their feelings and to express
affection to those whom they love.

R

RABBIT

YEARS OF BIRTH: 1915, 1927, 1939, 1951, 1963, 1975, 1987, 1999, 2011

WHO AM I?

NATURAL ENERGY	Yin
NATURAL ELEMENT	Wood
CORRESPONDING TIME	(Rabbit ascendant) 5 A.M.–7 A.M.
CORRESPONDING MONTH	March
CORRESPONDING DIRECTION	East
CORRESPONDING SEASON	Spring
CHARACTER TRAITS	Diplomatic, peaceful, sensitive, intuitive, reflective, refined, stylish, moderate, caring, quiet, friendly, alert, even-tempered, clever, sexy, intelligent
PERSONAL NEEDS	Rabbits need to take account of their delicate senses and seek a quiet, peaceful environment in which to rest and reflect.
LIFE CHALLENGES	To overcome a fear of change and take more risks in life

TEMPERAMENT

Rabbits are the intuitive diplomats of the Chinese zodiac. Blessed
with natural style and good taste, they devote many of their
resources to their attire and household goods. A secure and
harmonious environment is vital for the sensitive Rabbit. Rabbits
like to operate in the background, preferring to observe and reflect,
rather than being actively engaged. They will tactfully handle any
issue that arises and will effortlessly manage disputes, generally
achieving peaceful resolutions. They make able negotiators.

LOVE AND RELATIONSHIPS

Flexible and easy to get along with, Rabbits detest confrontations,
preferring to reason out any disagreements. As Rabbits are more
introverted than extroverted, they prefer the company of small,
intimate groups to large and exciting parties, enjoying entertaining
in style and at a leisurely pace. Their love of nature and curiosity

about the world make them keen travelers and flexible traveling companions.

Rabbits demonstrate a taste for the finer things in life when it comes to their homes. They have good taste and a keen eye for valuable objects. They are responsible and calm parents who go to great lengths to ensure harmonious relationships are maintained in the family. They have a calming influence and like to practice what they preach.

Rabbits are extremely sexy and irresistible in the affairs of the heart. Sensitive, indulgent, and romantic, they will invest much time and energy in their intimate relationships, expecting the same from their partners. They make lighthearted teasers who are attracted to older and wiser lovers, seeking security and protection.

WORK AND BUSINESS

Rabbits require autonomy and quiet surroundings in order to perform at their best. Independent roles suit them well, so they can operate at their own comfortable and even pace. Any occupation in the arts will suit them. Rabbits' intuition and intelligence also equip them well in the business world, where they would be especially successful as diplomats or mediators. In the workplace, Rabbits' flexibility and genuine concern for others ensure they can fit easily into any team. Ideal occupations include diplomat, antique dealer, interior decorator, art collector, sociologist, and mediator.

In Chinese astrology, each of the five elements—Metal, Water, Wood, Fire, and Earth—is dominant in a particular year. This imbues the animal associated with each year with a particular character.

- If you were born in 1915 or 1975, you are a **WOOD RABBIT**.
- If you were born in 1927 or 1987, you are a **FIRE RABBIT**.
- If you were born in 1939 or 1999, you are an **EARTH RABBIT**.
- If you were born in 1951 or 2011, you are a **METAL RABBIT**.
- If you were born in 1963, you are a **WATER RABBIT**.

RAT

●

YEARS OF BIRTH: 1912, 1924, 1936, 1948, 1960, 1972, 1984, 1996, 2008

WHO AM I?

NATURAL ENERGY	Yang
NATURAL ELEMENT	Water
CORRESPONDING TIME	(Rat ascendant) 11 P.M.–1 A.M.
CORRESPONDING MONTH	December
CORRESPONDING DIRECTION	North
CORRESPONDING SEASON	Winter
CHARACTER TRAITS	Intelligent, industrious, resourceful, practical, self-motivated, thrifty, charming, communicative, compassionate, calm, observant, analytical, caring, discreet
PERSONAL NEEDS	Rats need copious amounts of attention, recognition, and praise; otherwise, they will quickly focus their energies elsewhere to address their personal insecurities
LIFE CHALLENGES	To overcome their inner fears and insecurities and diminish their nervous anxiety

TEMPERAMENT

Rats are the resourceful masterminds of the Chinese zodiac. Highly communicative and endowed with abundant intelligence and financial acumen, they are driven by the desire to accumulate wealth to ensure their financial security. Their superior analytical skills guarantee them career success. They make excellent strategic partners in business, where they are motivated just as much by accolades as they are by financial reward. Being social creatures, rats are at home in groups and they love to entertain. Rats are perceived by others as tasteful and elegant, in an understated fashion.

LOVE AND RELATIONSHIPS

The considerate and supportive nature of rats makes them good friends. They like helping close friends where they can, with advice, personal coaching, or money. As rats value loyalty, they tend to have only a few close friends, although they do like being entertained by numerous acquaintances. Rats are particularly fond of praise and open demonstrations of appreciation. They are also loyal to those they care about.

Rats are excellent at providing for their families financially and take their responsibilities as caretakers seriously. They want to be leaders within their families, encouraging and supporting partners and children. They take a democratic approach to decision-making, but need to feel they have significant influence, if not control, within the home, particularly given their thrift, wisdom, and sensitivity.

Rats are innovative when it comes to wooing their chosen mates. Well equipped with quick wits, warm natures, and stylish grooming, Rats have great success as attentive and debonair lovers. While young, they are drawn to the challenge of artful seduction using their extensive interpersonal skills. However, it is the quality of a committed, long-term relationship they desire most and not a lifelong parade of superficial affairs. Once committed, they make gentle, loyal, and protective partners who will always take the time needed to nurture their relationships and support and care for their partners.

WORK AND BUSINESS

Rats are at home in the world of business. With a keen intellect and obvious competence, they seek occupations that engage them fully and make good use of their mental dexterity. They need visible recognition for their hard work to maintain their loyalty. Without adequate amounts of praise and recognition, rats can become insecure and unmotivated. Ideal occupations for rats include business director, accountant, stockbroker, courtroom lawyer, auctioneer, or politician.

In Chinese astrology, each of the five elements—Metal, Water, Wood, Fire, and Earth—is dominant in a particular year. This imbues the animal associated with each year with a particular character.

- If you were born in 1924 or 1984, you are a **WOOD RAT**.
- If you were born in 1936 or 1996, you are a **FIRE RAT**.
- If you were born in 1948 or 2008, you are an **EARTH RAT**.
- If you were born in 1960, you are a **METAL RAT**.
- If you were born in 1912 or 1972, you are a **WATER RAT**.

RAVEN

BIRTH DATES: Northern Hemisphere: September 23 to October 22
Southern Hemisphere: March 21 to April 19

WHO AM I?

BIRTH TIME ANIMAL TOTEM	Raven
BIRTH TIME ELEMENT	Air
ELEMENTAL CLAN	Butterfly
ENERGY FLOW	Active
LIFE PATH	To explore and comprehend humanity's inner darkness and then to act as the communication medium between the physical and spiritual worlds for others
PERSONAL GIFTS	Intelligence, insight, intuition, inspiration, diplomacy, influence, adaptability, resourcefulness
PERSONAL CHALLENGES	Depression, indecision, confusion, manipulation
CORRESPONDING SEASON	Early fall (autumn)—a time of browning and falling leaves and the shortening of days
SEASONAL ELEMENT	Earth
SEASONAL TOTEM	Grizzly Bear
COLOR	Brown
PLANT	Mullein
GEMSTONE	Bloodstone jasper

RAVEN PEOPLE

Ravens, as black as night itself, are said by Native Americans to possess magical powers. Their medicine is rather strong: sighting one is a message to turn and face your inner darkness and your fears, and transform your life.

Raven people are extraordinarily special individuals, as they act as natural catalysts for the transformation of other people's lives. They are especially intuitive and diplomatic, demonstrating great care and consideration for their fellow humans. They are generally open-hearted, charming, and peace-loving people who demonstrate exceptional communication and listening skills.

Ravens have a strong social conscience, which can lead them to be overly idealistic at times. As they are good at starting things, you will often find them working tirelessly behind the scenes to influence those in power, getting them to restore and maintain harmony and peace within their communities.

Raven people tend to dislike solitude, preferring the company of others, whether in a social, business, or personal context. Physically attractive and affectionate, they need to give and receive physical affection regularly, otherwise, they could slip into a depressive or confused emotional state that would all too easily disrupt their harmonious natures.

At their best, Raven people are quite in tune with their physical and emotional sides. This leaves only one real challenge—to develop their latent psychic abilities. If they do so, they could be of much greater service to others, as healers or as psychic mediums.

ELEMENTAL CLAN

As their birth time element is Air, Ravens belong to the Butterfly clan. Butterflies are colorful and graceful. They begin life as caterpillars, only to be transformed into their beautiful and free-flowing state after an intense, cocoon-wrapped metamorphosis. To Native Americans, they are a symbol of change, transformation, and hope.

Like the butterfly, Raven people are beautiful and delightful to have around. They are active, energetic and ever-changing, in physical appearance as well as in their feelings, thoughts, and opinions. As such, they have the power to transform and uplift those around them. They are intelligent, innovative, and expressive individuals. But their appearance and behavior can be most deceiving, even to themselves. If they are nurtured and respected, they will remain calm and refreshing. If they are angered, they may quickly erupt into an overpowering fury.

SEASONAL ELEMENT

Your seasonal totem animal, the Grizzly Bear, is closely related to the element governing the season in which you were born. For more information about your seasonal totem animal and your seasonal element, Earth, see pages 78–79.

> • *Strengths to cultivate* Flexibility, spirituality, optimism, humanitarianism • *Possible weaknesses to address* Lack of practicality and perseverance, a lack of control in emotional responses

ROOSTER •

YEARS OF BIRTH: 1921, 1933, 1945, 1957, 1969, 1981, 1993, 2005, 2017

WHO AM I?

NATURAL ENERGY	Yin
NATURAL ELEMENT	Metal
CORRESPONDING TIME	(Rooster ascendant) 5 P.M.–7 P.M.
CORRESPONDING MONTH	September
CORRESPONDING DIRECTION	West
CORRESPONDING SEASON	Fall
CHARACTER TRAITS	Flamboyant, resourceful, courageous, resilient, cultivated, capable, entertaining, critical, proud, knowledgeable, ambitious, frank, extravagant, protective, impulsive, provocative
PERSONAL NEEDS	Roosters need a special place in their homes to relax and collect their wits and also the understanding of their family members when they are too brash.
LIFE CHALLENGES	To believe truly in themselves and rely less on others' opinions

TEMPERAMENT

Roosters are spirited, fearless, proud individuals who speak their minds and are meticulous in their dress. They are flashy, jumping at every opportunity to socialize and entertain. Desiring the limelight, they love being center stage. As they are so keen on appearances, Roosters can be overly sensitive to the criticism of others. However, underneath all the bright feathers, they are extremely intelligent. Blessed with acute perception and a yearning for knowledge, they are scrupulous in their attention to detail and have extraordinarily high standards. A Rooster's life is anything but dull.

LOVE AND RELATIONSHIPS

Roosters love company and will frequently entertain. They have a vast array of friends and acquaintances. Their homes are highly decorative, immaculately clean, and probably too big for their needs. Sensitive to the opinions of others, Roosters constantly seek feedback from their most trusted friends and can place too much value on their judgments. They are generous with their time and possessions. In their much-needed quiet time, Roosters will indulge their private passion of reading.

Living with a Rooster can be hard work, as they want their family members to shine in every situation. They set high standards for themselves, their partners, and their children, who can fall short of the mark. Roosters will also get into great debt to finance what they consider to be just the right home. They can be very direct but are also protective and generous with loved ones and will give freely of their time to support them.

Roosters like to be in control of all their relationships and to be showered with praise, feeding their secret insecurities. They are renowned as skilled lovers with stamina. Focused on their own performance, Roosters come across as a little self-obsessed to their lovers. In an attempt to win approval, they can be very generous and romantic.

WORK AND BUSINESS

Roosters love tradition, pomp, and ceremony, and will be attracted to any occupation in uniform—particularly if they can be adorned with medals and awards. As they are so focused on outward appearances, they will be impressed by titles and high rank. Yet they have natural talents that often go unnoticed, such as a love of hard work and attention to detail. Ideal occupations for Roosters include television presenter, military officer, public relations officer, salesperson, critic, academic, actor, model, or police officer.

In Chinese astrology, each of the five elements—Metal, Water, Wood, Fire, and Earth—is dominant in a particular year. This imbues the animal associated with each year with a particular character.

If you were born in 1945 or 2005, you are a **WOOD ROOSTER**.

If you were born in 1957 or 2017, you are a **FIRE ROOSTER**.

If you were born in 1969, you are an **EARTH ROOSTER**.

If you were born in 1921 or 1981, you are a **METAL ROOSTER**.

If you were born in 1933 or 1993, you are a **WATER ROOSTER**.

S

SAGITTARIUS

BIRTH DATES: November 22 to December 21

WHO AM I?

SYMBOL	*The Archer* *Sagittarius' dual nature of half-man and half-beast*
QUEST	*Exploration*
RULING PLANET	*Jupiter* *Expansion, opportunity, good fortune, luck, optimism, wealth*
RULING ELEMENT	*Fire* *Enthusiasm, confidence, passion, energy*
POLARITY	*Positive* *Impulsivity, excitability, communicativeness, sociability*
QUALITY	*Mutable* *Adaptability, flexibility, cohesiveness*
COLOR	*Light blue* *Clarity*
FOOD	*Spinach, eggplant sage, allspice, clove, figs*
FLOWER	*Chrysanthemum, holly, magnolia*
HEALING HERB	*Chervil, sage* *In old herbal lore, the leaves of chervil were said to be helpful to Sagittarians suffering from rheumatism.*
GEMSTONE	*Turquoise* *Luck and love*
SUITABLE GIFTS	*Jewelry featuring turquoise or amethyst; an active vacation; red candles; sports equipment*

TEMPERAMENT

Sagittarius is the adventurous, freedom-loving sign of the zodiac. Sagittarians constantly need movement, excitement, and change. This can create a general restlessness and reluctance to commit to long-range plans. Sagittarians are happy-go-lucky and fun loving. They take risks and enjoy danger, which means they can sometimes live to regret their decisions and actions.

Sagittarians are invariably lucky, having a definite knack for being in the right place at the right time. They also tend to attract good fortune through their undeniable capacity for hard work.

Moreover, Sagittarians possess a fine instinct for opportunity, a talent they appreciate and come to rely on increasingly.

Those born under the sign of Sagittarius are generally personable and likable people. They enjoy significant personal power, both socially and professionally, simply through being themselves. In particular, those born on or around December 6 are downright charming: bright, cheerful, chatty, and enthusiastic about everything life has to offer. All Sagittarians are typically loyal, fearless, farsighted, and often blessed with remarkably fine judgment (although they may be a little hot-headed or impulsive at times).

Like the mythical archer, Sagittarians are also strong individuals in their own right. They rarely lean upon others and usually think carefully before making a major decision or embarking on any significant activity. But they are very action-oriented, rather than passive. Sagittarians are often those who initiate or generate response in others. As adults, they often demonstrate considerable talent as speakers, teachers, lecturers, or trainers.

Personal areas that Sagittarians may consider working on include tactfulness, timing, and objective analysis.

LOVE AND RELATIONSHIPS

It may seem something of a contradiction, given the above, that the Sagittarian is the person most able and most likely to live alone.

However, Sagittarians adore their families and take special interest in their children's education. They are also generous and helpful to their partners.

As a rule, Sagittarians have extremely high personal, moral, and ethical standards, demanding the same high standards of others that they do of themselves. This profoundly important aspect of their nature leads them to be unsparing in their judgment of others and very sparing in terms of forgiveness.

Sagittarians are not likely to forgive, nor are they likely to forget if someone is guilty of transgressing the bounds of decent, civilized behavior, particularly with the family or friends of a Sagittarian. In the case of Sagittarians born on or near December 1, any such falling out may be marked by drastic action on their part. An angry impulse on the part of a fired-up Sagittarian with a December 1 birth date may result in an argument, culminating in the permanent severing of communications. With most other Sagittarians, however, such a break would be equally irrevocable, but civil to a degree well below freezing point.

In addition to sharing the Sagittarian's high ethical standards, the ideal partner should be affable and easygoing, someone who will not want to share the Sagittarian's limelight and who will not in any way compete for the admiration the admirable and even quite dazzlingly attractive Sagittarian is used to receiving from the rest of the world. It will help if Sagittarians' partners are good communicators, intelligent and articulate, and enjoy discussing matters of worldly import and particular interest to the Sagittarian. Many Sagittarians will be more than delighted if their partner is simply an ideal listener.

WORK AND BUSINESS

Sagittarians make optimistic and enthusiastic work colleagues. Any occupation that provides freedom of thought and/or travel will suit them. Their restlessness can result in frequent job changes, and many  will not find their niches until later in life. Sagittarians enjoy large projects, and many of them are excellent builders and handypersons. They prefer a skilled type of job that takes them from place to place and allows them to meet a number of different people.

Sagittarians tend to gravitate toward occupations that allow for plenty of dynamism and movement, both physically and intellectually. Sales, travel, and the armed services are all likely to appeal to them. Of all the signs, they tend to have the greatest regard for human rights and the goodness inherent in humanity. This may lead them to work to improve peace and understanding at either a community or a world level.

Sagittarians work best in open environments with as few rules and restrictions as possible. They need constant challenges and change in order to focus their energy and quench their thirst for variety. Any outdoor environment will suit, and nontraditional working environments are exciting to them.

Sagittarians make eager and optimistic leaders. They like to be kept busy with many different projects at once, and will ensure their staff are doing the same. They have a knack for boosting office morale, sharing their opinions, and delegating the more mundane tasks. Their honorable character and clear conviction as to what is and is not acceptable behavior attract unswerving loyalty from others. The Sagittarian boss will frequently be absent from the office, taking up every opportunity for overseas or interstate travel.

BLENDING THE SYSTEMS

Sagittarians born in November

The Fire sign of Sagittarius denotes that November Sagittarians have an enthusiastic, humorous, generous personality. Their need for freedom means they will choose a job that takes them out and about—this can delay marriage and parenthood until later in life. Their Chinese sign, the receptive Water Pig, makes them deeper and more intellectual than outsiders might realize. This lends an artistic and musical streak, as well as a sense of timing where business matters are concerned. Their Native American sign is the stately Elk of the Thunderbird clan, which makes them quiet when young, but more outgoing later. This sign gives them a strong sense of justice. Elk people are outwardly friendly, but secretive about their deepest feelings.

Sagittarians born in December

December Sagittarians need freedom in both their personal relationships and their working life. The Chinese sign for December is the active Water Rat, which allows them to succeed against appalling odds. The active Water element adds commercial and financial sense. Their Native American sign is the Elk of the Thunderbird clan, which gives them a regal air and a tendency to keep their feelings hidden.

SALMON

BIRTH DATES: Northern Hemisphere: July 23 to August 22
Southern Hemisphere: January 20 to February 18

WHO AM I?

BIRTH TIME ANIMAL TOTEM	Salmon
BIRTH TIME ELEMENT	Fire
ELEMENTAL CLAN	Thunderbird
ENERGY FLOW	Active
LIFE PATH	To harness the vital energies that can surge through you, in order to achieve emotional balance and harmony with your environment
PERSONAL GIFTS	Energy, versatility, sensuality, benevolence, determination, affection, charm, courage
PERSONAL CHALLENGES	Impulsiveness, arrogance, selfishness, greed
CORRESPONDING SEASON	Heart of summer—a time of ripening, of reaching growth potential
SEASONAL ELEMENT	Water
SEASONAL TOTEM	Coyote
COLOR	Red
PLANT	Raspberry
GEMSTONE	Garnet

SALMON PEOPLE

In the wild, salmon are required to swim back upstream, against the rushing currents, to find their spawning grounds. Native Americans respect them for their vital energy and determination. Sighting salmon on their trek upstream is a reminder to us to take stock of our own vital energies to ensure they are kept in control and directed positively.

Salmon people are outgoing, action-oriented people who find it difficult to slow their hectic daily pace. They are robust and usually seem larger than life. Gregarious and versatile, they are bombastic when communicating. At the very least, Salmon people always stand out in a crowd.

At their best, Salmon people appear friendly and charming, never failing to entertain in social settings. At their worst, they can be erratic, even impulsive, and hot-tempered and almost vengeful if they allow their emotions to run unchecked.

When the situation calls for courage, Salmon people are usually first in line. This makes them naturally suited to leadership roles, where their big-hearted and magnanimous approach to others can be widely appreciated.

Salmon people are also sensually active. They take pride in their appearance and even more in their sexual prowess. They sometimes need to curb their personal desires in order to ensure that selfishness and greed do not take control of their actions and in the process misdirect their honor and integrity.

ELEMENTAL CLAN

As their birth time element is Fire, Salmon people belong to the Thunderbird clan. A Native American myth tells how the thunderbird, the largest and most magnificent of the Hawks, fell prey to arrogance, developing an inflated ego. In a burst of fire from a thunderbolt sent by the Creator, it was raised from the earth to become a spirit. Like the thunderbird, Salmon people are powerful, radiant, and passionate. They have spirited and enthusiastic personalities, and thrive on activity and change. They are charming and witty people who love being the center of attention, delighting in acknowledgment and praise from others. Just like fire, their emotions can vary in the extreme, from warm to blazing.

SEASONAL ELEMENT

Your seasonal totem animal, the Coyote, is closely related to the element governing the season in which you were born. For more information about your seasonal totem animal and your seasonal element, Water, see pages 178–179.

• **Strengths to cultivate** Intuition, physical stamina, optimism, motivation • **Possible weaknesses to address** Gullibility to flattery, inflated ego, oversensitivity to constructive criticism

SCORPIO ●

BIRTH DATES: October 23 to November 21

WHO AM I?

SYMBOL	*The scorpion* Scorpio's deep and mysterious emotions and strong instincts
QUEST	*Transformation*
RULING PLANET	*Pluto* Regeneration, transformation, evolution, rebirth
RULING ELEMENT	Water Emotion and sensitivity
POLARITY	*Negative* Receptivity, sensitivity, reserve, the desire for privacy
QUALITY	*Fixed* Stability, loyalty, endurance
COLOR	*Black* A lucky color for the strongly individual and independent Scorpio
FOOD	*Asparagus, carrots, leeks, onions, coriander, cranberry*
FLOWER	*Marigold, chrysanthemum, honeysuckle*
HEALING HERB	*Basil, stinging nettle, tarragon*
GEMSTONE	*Topaz* Wealth, success, protection against danger
SUITABLE GIFTS	Jewelry featuring topaz or pearls, fine housewares, gourmet cookware, nonfiction books on their current favorite topics

TEMPERAMENT

Scorpio is the intensely mysterious, impenetrable sign of the zodiac. Driven by their secret desires and a need for emotional fulfillment, Scorpios can shift from being passionate and sensual one minute to being icy cold and indifferent the next. Scorpios take a focused and totally committed approach to everything. Their mental radar and highly developed probing skills ensure that little escapes their attention and critical assessment.

While their passion for life makes Scorpios fascinating and disarming lovers, partners, and friends, the sting in their tails is their love of freedom. Those born under the influence of Scorpio tend to chafe under any other influence. If not the maestro conducting the orchestra, then Scorpio is a soloist.

Whether predominantly introverted or extroverted—and Scorpios can be either—those born under this sign generally look at life as an exciting adventure and seek stimulus from many sources.

Those born on November 4 are truly powerful personalities and may pursue careers that entail public performance or presentation. They will usually experience happiness in love and worldly success, which complements the tenacious, forceful, and ambitious nature of the typical Scorpio. Scorpios born in the middle of the sign, between October 31 and November 2, are blessed with a fertile imagination that fuels their quite extraordinary talent for organization on a large scale.

All Scorpios can be impulsive and exhibit a pioneering spirit and love of travel. They are sensualists who revel in food, wine, art, music, perfumes, and fine linens. All are expert at finding a dozen little ways in which to indulge themselves every day, sometimes secretly. They can also become greedy materialists on a higher level—they may have a voracious hunger for knowledge, which leads them to devour books or complete courses of study in record time. Often they combine pleasure with the generous and philanthropic side of their natures, finding pleasure in a good cause.

Personal areas that Scorpios may consider developing include easing up on self-criticism and sharing more of themselves with others.

LOVE AND RELATIONSHIPS

Life is interesting for the partner of a Scorpio. One of Scorpios' basic inclinations is to suspect others of wishing to control them.

Patient indeed must be the one who loves a Scorpio. Scorpios are often very free with wildly exaggerated opinions and prepared to argue.

They can hurt their friends and lovers quite badly, for they have the meanest temper of all the signs. Scorpios born toward the beginning of the sign tend to have more control over their temper, letting their anger burn like a dry-ice chill. Those born on or around October 29 may need to learn to control an almost savage temper. However, Scorpios are also tender-hearted, and when remorseful, will go to great lengths to make amends.

WORK AND BUSINESS

Scorpios harbor a desire to succeed and can patiently work away in the background to satisfy their long-held ambitions. They are passionate about precision and have a knack for problem-solving and focusing their attention in the most challenging of situations.

Whatever their career choice, Scorpios are more inclined to excel when they are not tied to a team. But to maintain their motivation, they must be sure their purpose is valuable, they have plenty of

stimulus and variety in their work, and they are supported by trusted staff. Scorpio people should select business partners who are good planners and organizers, for while Scorpios hold the big picture in view with no trouble at all, they tend to ignore details, often regarding them as minor.

Scorpios, true to their namesake's aptitude for survival, have a great knack for making the best out of unfortunate situations. They are also more than likely to make good circumstances even better, often to the point of excellence. In their business and professional lives, they are shrewd and observant, with a keen eye for new trends and unexplored opportunities, profitable alternatives, and byways, by-products, and spin-offs.

A secure and functional environment is the ideal of Scorpios. Hospitals and scientific and medical laboratories attract them. Their offices hold textbooks and journals and the latest in technological equipment. They prefer to work independently rather than in a team, but are skilled at shutting out distractions if working with others nearby is necessary.

Scorpio bosses are spirited and intuitive. They demand competence and loyalty from their staff and will quickly discard those who do not meet the mark. Scorpios are extremely skilled at general management positions involving all areas of business. Scorpio bosses in these roles will be able to use their talent for organizational strategy and transformation.

The Scorpio person usually has great physical stamina, and this, together with the Scorpio capacity for survival, can cause Scorpios to push themselves too hard, too fast, and too far. And, just as Scorpios are contradictory and secretive people, so their stamina may belie some internal weakness. Many naturopaths believe Scorpios are particularly vulnerable to complications of the circulatory, reproductive, and urinary organs.

BLENDING THE SYSTEMS

Scorpio born in October

The Water sign of Scorpio is noted for its power. Many military and political leaders come under this sign, but so do gifted homemakers and hardworking employees. The Chinese sign is the active Earth Dog, which can make October Scorpios naive and sentimental but also extremely helpful and hardworking. Their creative talent means they can work with their hands as well as their minds. Their Native American sign is the Serpent of the Frog clan, which indicates intelligence, but can also mean an extremely bad temper. October Scorpios can adapt themselves to most circumstances when they need to.

Scorpio born in November

The Water sign of Scorpio knows no middle way, so November Scorpios' loves and hates are equally intense, and their opinions are strong. The Chinese sign for this month is the Pig, which makes the Scorpio person look mild while hiding an acute mind. The receptive Water aspect ensures that November Scorpios' head for business is allied to a love of the arts. They are happier working behind the scenes than out in front. Their Native American sign is the Serpent of the Frog clan, which means they have a talent for teaching, along with the ability to transform their life when the need arises. This changes to the Elk of the Thunderbird clan, which indicates they have a regal air, a great deal of insight, and teaching ability.

SEVEN

Birth numbers or personal destiny numbers are easy to calculate. Discarding all zeros, total your date, month, and year of birth and reduce that figure to one digit. For example, if you were born on June 27, 1960, number four would be your personal destiny number: $6 + 2 + 7 + 1 + 9 + 6 = 31 = 3 + 1 = 4$.

WHO AM I?

GENERAL CHARACTERISTICS	Number Seven is intellectual, philosophical, imaginative, and overemotional
RULING PLANET	Neptune
ELEMENT	Water
COLORS	Green
GEMSTONES	Moonstone

TEMPERAMENT

As seven is one of the more significant numbers in magic and mysticism, those who have it as their birth number are often otherworldly, intuitive, sensitive individuals. Their primary interests will usually be philosophy, spirituality and the supernatural, and religion—often that of cultures other than their own.

Sevens prefer a quiet, orderly life, and are usually happier reading or communing with nature than having a busy social life. Many Sevens are highly psychic and find the presence of crowds overwhelming. Their interests and contentment with their own company may result in their being considered eccentric, but they may secretly enjoy this reputation.

The emotional sensitivity of most Sevens often means their state of mind has a strong influence on their physical health. Nervous tension, depression, or even just one of life's disappointments can often send their health downhill, the kidneys and urinary system are the areas commonly affected. Sevens should be particularly conscientious about drinking a healthy amount of water each day.

Sevens are also prone to conditions of the lungs, eyes, nose and skin that are exacerbated by allergies. Sevens suffering from illnesses such as asthma or sinusitis should check their environments and diets for factors that exacerbate these conditions. Similarly, those inclined to rashes or other skin problems should be allergy tested to discover whether any causes can be found in their food, choice of fabrics, or cleaning products.

While the world needs dreamers, Sevens sometimes live the role too fully, to the point of making a virtue of their impracticality. At its most dangerous, this can turn to self-delusion. More often, it merely grates on their more pragmatic friends and colleagues. Sevens will occasionally use their reputations as romantic visionaries to justify laziness, indecision, evasiveness, or a refusal to accept responsibility.

Oversensitive to the harshness of the world, they often deliberately keep it at a distance, only to indulge in self-pity and a sense of having been abandoned by others. Alternatively, they may become overly critical of their friends and consider them unreasonable if they protest. Sevens may require a gentle reminder now and then that they do not have exclusive rights to sensitivity.

LOVE AND RELATIONSHIPS

Having high standards in all things, Sevens look for quality rather than quantity in their relationships. Often shy and remote, they mix best with people of a similar nature or those who can gently encourage them out of their shell. In both friendships and partnerships, Sevens need a strong spiritual aspect and find those who live their lives purely on the material dimension puzzling.

Imaginative and thoughtful, Sevens enjoy romance, but need to retain a certain amount of emotional privacy. This can sometimes be misinterpreted by partners as intentional secretiveness. Sevens are also inclined to spend energy analyzing every aspect of their relationships, attempting to foresee and avoid pitfalls. This will often have the effect of creating problems where none had previously existed.

WORK AND BUSINESS

Sevens are often uncomfortable in careers that require them to work as part of a large body of employees, preferring positions in which much of their time is spent alone or with only one or two individuals. Since their strengths are in sensitivity, observation, and analysis, they will often excel in fields such as psychology, psychiatry, counseling, and various other healing therapies.

Many Sevens work in biological research (particularly marine biology), astronomy, or any field that requires solitude in the natural environment. Those who prefer a roof over their heads while working are likely to seek jobs in libraries, bookstores, museums, galleries, and the academic world.

SHEEP ●

YEARS OF BIRTH: 1919, 1931, 1943, 1955, 1967, 1979, 1991, 2003, 2015

WHO AM I?

NATURAL ENERGY	Yin
NATURAL ELEMENT	Earth
CORRESPONDING TIME	(Sheep ascendant) 1 P.M.–3 P.M.
CORRESPONDING MONTH	July
CORRESPONDING DIRECTION	South/Southwest
CORRESPONDING SEASON	Late summer
CHARACTER TRAITS	Creative, imaginative, sensitive, sincere, cautious, adaptable, gentle, easygoing, refined, moderate, calm, optimistic, orderly, friendly, romantic, sympathetic, pleasant, honest
PERSONAL NEEDS	Sheep need a supportive, stress-free environment at home and at work.
LIFE CHALLENGES	To develop confidence in their own abilities and take more risks in life

TEMPERAMENT

Sheep are the peacemakers of the Chinese zodiac. Calm by nature, they are pacifists and will recoil from any confrontation. They are also quiet, friendly, patient, and extremely adaptable, and get along with others very easily. They make good listeners and are sympathetic friends. Highly principled, sensitive, and artistically talented, Sheep will often find their calling in the fields of music, literature, or art. Here they revel in being left alone, free of the influence of others, to express their imagination.

LOVE AND RELATIONSHIPS

As peacemakers and generous spirits, Sheep are valuable friends who feel acutely the need to support friends both emotionally and financially. They are loyal and totally accepting of differences, and expect their friends to be there when their own situations call for a shoulder to cry on. While they like to socialize and are very good at bringing people together, Sheep frequently need time alone to rest and rejuvenate.

Sheep love being part of a group, and a close-knit family is ideal. Once married, they cherish the continued security and closeness and go to great lengths to ensure the family's emotional stability and harmony. Sheep homes are full of warmth and love. Naturals in the parental role, Sheep are patient and skilled at nurturing and communicating with young minds. The security and stability of family life can act as a source of inspiration and support to fuel their creative talents.

Sheep are sensuous, with very active sex drives. They are in tune with their own feelings and desires, and intuitive about their partners' needs. Compassionate and understanding, Sheep are romantic and expect generosity and attention. They can express their own needs and desires and ensure they are met. Once committed, Sheep make faithful and considerate partners.

WORK AND BUSINESS

Sheep are popular at work with employers and colleagues alike and take a flexible, friendly, easygoing approach to work and work relationships. Not excessively career-oriented, Sheep are happy to remain involved in people issues or creative pursuits rather than politics. They are good with details and at analyzing problem areas. Sheep may be particular with their own work, and others may perceive them as perfectionists. They need a supportive, stress-free work environment in order to perform and frequently fall ill if their workplace becomes chaotic. Ideal occupations for Sheep include being a writer, poet, musician, artist, actor, therapist, religious minister, architect, or gardener.

In Chinese astrology, each of the five elements—Metal, Water, Wood, Fire, and Earth—is dominant in a particular year. This imbues the animal associated with each year with a particular character.

- If you were born in 1955 or 2015, you are a **WOOD SHEEP**.
- If you were born in 1967, you are a **FIRE SHEEP**.
- If you were born in 1919 or 1979, you are an **EARTH SHEEP**.
- If you were born in 1931 or 1991, you are a **METAL SHEEP**.
- If you were born in 1943 or 2003, you are a **WATER SHEEP**.

SIX ●

Birth numbers or personal destiny numbers are easy to calculate. Discarding all zeros, total your date, month, and year of birth and reduce that figure to one digit. For example, if you were born on June 27, 1960, number four would be your personal destiny number: $6 + 2 + 7 + 1 + 9 + 6 = 31 = 3 + 1 = 4$.

WHO AM I?

GENERAL CHARACTERISTICS	Number Six is romantic, creative, compassionate, and family-oriented.
RULING PLANET	Venus
ELEMENT	Earth
COLORS	Green, blue
GEMSTONES	Emerald

TEMPERAMENT

Those whose birth number is six are very giving, warm-hearted individuals who place a high value on domestic bliss. Their homes are their centers—many Sixes either work from home or aspire to do so, and just as many find that their home becomes a place where their friends often gather. They spend much of their time ensuring that their living environments are sanctuaries of peace, companionship, and beauty.

Artistic themselves, Sixes also find great pleasure in the work of other creative people. Consequently they are often collectors of art, antiques, and music, or connoisseurs of wine and food. They have an excellent dress sense.

Sixes are often among the healthiest of people, since food preparation and healthy nutrition are of great interest to them. Their fondness for luxury occasionally leads them into overindulgence, but they are usually quick to restore the balance. Many Sixes make a study of the field, becoming very competent amateur or even professional dieticians. This is fortunate, since Sixes are also traditionally prone to digestive, heart, and circulation problems, all of which would be alleviated by a wholesome diet. Many Sixes find a vegetarian diet suits their constitutions best, while others will develop their own forms of food combination for maximum benefit. Their tenderhearted natures can cause Sixes to worry excessively about others' welfare, leading to stress-related ailments, but daily exercise can keep these at bay.

Sixes' love for domesticity makes them guard it jealously. They are particularly vulnerable if their family or relationship with their partner is under threat. At such times they are more likely to engage in self-destructive behavior than aggression, overindulging in comfort food, alcohol, or pure self-pity.

Their inherent generosity is often exploited by others. They find it difficult to decline requests for help, but may end up begrudging the amount of time this eats up. This resentment usually goes unexpressed, but Sixes often broadcast this through a general air of martyrdom in the hope it will be noticed. Perfectionists by nature, Sixes also need to guard against being excessively critical of themselves and others.

LOVE AND RELATIONSHIPS

Sixes, with their nurturing and compassionate natures, have little trouble winning friends who recognize that Sixes are people on whom they can rely for support in any situation. Always family oriented, Sixes often see their friends as extended family and treat them accordingly.

Sixes love the atmosphere and trimmings of romance, which can sometimes lead them to commit themselves to a relationship too eagerly. Consequently, they may have a few false starts before settling on a really suitable partner. Once a strong, stable relationship has been formed, Sixes dedicate themselves to it wholeheartedly. Their affectionate nature makes them aware of the charms of others, but Sixes are typically very loyal to their partners and very disinclined to risk their domestic happiness by entering into flirtations or flings.

WORK AND BUSINESS

Sixes can usually work equally well as part of a team or by themselves, with many dividing their time between the two options. They are generally happiest when they can use their considerable artistic flair in their careers. Many find work as musicians, interior decorators, jewelers, or photographers, or within the fashion industry. Others become professional writers, designers, or artists, often in a freelance capacity to allow them to work from home offices.

Their inclination to nurture others makes them ideally suited to psychology, counseling, social welfare work, and community care. The same instinct leads some Sixes into the hospitality industry, professional cookery, or catering.

SNAKE

●

YEARS OF BIRTH: 1917, 1929, 1941, 1953, 1965, 1977, 1989, 2001, 2013

WHO AM I?

NATURAL ENERGY	Yin
NATURAL ELEMENT	Fire
CORRESPONDING TIME	(Snake ascendant) 9 A.M.–11 A.M.
CORRESPONDING MONTH	May
CORRESPONDING DIRECTION	South/Southeast
CORRESPONDING SEASON	Early summer
CHARACTER TRAITS	Alert, intelligent, intuitive, wise, calculating, conservative, cautious, mysterious, alluring, elegant, shrewd, sophisticated, sensual, reflective, organized
PERSONAL NEEDS	Snakes need to know they can influence others and receive respect for the advice they give. They need to be told how clever they are and how beneficial their counsel has been.
LIFE CHALLENGES	To become more physically involved in their world, and more emotionally accessible

TEMPERAMENT

Snake people have a serene presence and rarely reveal feelings of agitation or stress. They are self-disciplined and fond of tradition. Given their perceptive minds, natural sophistication, and reflective natures, Snakes are often sought after for their opinions and counsel. They make skilled negotiators and will swiftly distinguish themselves in any position of influence. Snakes are true intellectuals, preferring the world of thought to the world of action. Cultured and sophisticated, Snakes are conservative yet tasteful and are able to acquire material wealth easily.

LOVE AND RELATIONSHIPS

Snakes are the skilled networkers of the Chinese zodiac. They make use of every social gathering to develop contacts and are adept at camouflaging their intent. They do build honest friendships with others—but they seem to get more use out of their alliances than just friendship. They prefer artistic and cultural gatherings to sports or overly active, competitive gatherings. Snakes appreciate the finer things in life and will enjoy luxuriating in opulence. Fine dining and vintage wines are always popular with Snakes, who will hold many understated, but exquisite, formal dinner parties.

Snakes cherish their homes for the stability and protection they provide. They spend a lot of time and energy on creating just the right home environment. They are gifted with money management skills and will ensure that their families do not want for anything. Once settled, they make caring parents who are sensitive to their children's and partner's needs.

Snakes like to settle down quickly with someone they perceive can meet their high personal and social criteria. Given their clear agenda in matters of the heart, they can come across as cool and distant. However, once committed, they are capable of deep and enduring love for their partners.

WORK AND BUSINESS

Snakes are assured of professional success, given their ability to detach emotionally from situations and their adaptability. They do not necessarily seek obvious positions of power, preferring roles where they can influence and counsel the figureheads on strategic directions. Their business acumen and intuition will ensure they never fall prey to corporate traps. Snakes often find success later in life, as they may spend their younger years cultivating their social and artistic interests. Once they become career-oriented, Snakes demonstrate keen business acumen and political shrewdness. They have excellent organizational skills and are extremely efficient at everything they do. Ideal occupations for Snakes include scientist, academic, art or food critic, writer, poet, philosopher, human resource manager, or interior designer.

In Chinese astrology, each of the five elements—Metal, Water, Wood , Fire, and Earth—is dominant in a particular year. This imbues the animal associated with each year with a particular character.

- If you were born in 1965, you are a **WOOD SNAKE**.
- If you were born in 1917 or 1977, you are a **FIRE SNAKE**.
- If you were born in 1929 or 1989, you are an **EARTH SNAKE**.
- If you were born in 1941 or 2001, you are a **METAL SNAKE**.
- If you were born in 1953 or 2013, you are a **WATER SNAKE**.

SNAKE

BIRTH DATES: Northern Hemisphere: October 23 to November 21
Southern Hemisphere: April 20 to May 20

WHO AM I?

BIRTH TIME ANIMAL TOTEM	Snake
BIRTH TIME ELEMENT	Water
ELEMENTAL CLAN	Frog
ENERGY FLOW	Receptive
LIFE PATH	To take a dose of one's own medicine regularly, to stop resisting changing the self, and to go within regularly to experience one's own animal totem power of transformation
PERSONAL GIFTS	Patience, sensuality, ambition, charisma, wisdom, detachment, imagination, vitality
PERSONAL CHALLENGES	Jealousy, deceitfulness, stubbornness, a critical nature
CORRESPONDING SEASON	The heart of fall (autumn)—a time of early morning frosts and the coming of the cold
SEASONAL ELEMENT	Earth
SEASONAL TOTEM	Grizzly Bear
COLOR	Orange
PLANT	Thistle
GEMSTONE OR MINERAL	Copper

SNAKE PEOPLE

Snakes represent many things to Native Americans. First, they are seen as the ultimate transformative creatures, given their ability to shed their skins to suit their environment. This also demonstrates their superior survival skills. In addition, Snakes are prized for their sensual, hypnotic influence and are therefore often associated with physical desirability and procreation.

Snake people are said to have survived many trials in previous lives and, accordingly, to have earned the right to be linked to this auspicious animal totem. To have survived a Snake bite is a sign of having passed a physical and/or spiritual test. Therefore, Snake people are hardy, physically and mentally strong, and durable. They are life's real survivors and can regenerate quickly after setbacks.

Their keen observation skills and sensory acumen provide Snake people with insights into other people and environments that few can match. Snake people are the most skilled catalysts of change in others and in external events. However, this also means that Snake people are more resistant to changing themselves. They are determined and patient and have intense self-control.

Snake people tend to have highly charged sex drives, often hinted at by their physical intensity, smoldering sensuality and striking good looks. For Snake people to meet their sensual needs and fulfill their desires requires much of their significant reserve of physical and emotional energy.

Snake people are ambitious, usually acquiring success and wealth easily. They are driven to accumulate things such as money and possessions, but also like to accumulate new people and life experiences.

ELEMENTAL CLAN

As their birth time element is Water, Snakes belong to the Frog clan. The Frog is a very distinctive and adaptable creature. Its body is slick and nimble, and this gives it much agility and flexibility. The metamorphosis from tadpole to adult Frog demonstrates its ability to transform itself. Like the Frog, Snake people are very flexible and emotionally fluid individuals who possess the ability to transform themselves to suit their environments. The Water element provides them with creativity and expressiveness, making them skilled communicators. Their ideas and innovations have the capacity to transform people and environments, provided they can set clear directions and apply the discipline required for reaching their goals.

SEASONAL ELEMENT

Your seasonal totem animal, the Grizzly Bear, is closely related to the element governing the season in which you were born. For more information about your seasonal totem animal and your seasonal element, Earth, see pages 78–79.

• *Strengths to cultivate* Empathy, communication, creativity, emotional accessibility • *Possible weaknesses to address* Repression of emotions, stagnation of ideas, lack of discipline, an inability to change emotional responses

---

SNOW GOOSE

BIRTH DATES: Northern Hemisphere: December 22 to January 19
Southern Hemisphere: June 21 to July 22

WHO AM I?

BIRTH TIME ANIMAL TOTEM	Snow Goose
BIRTH TIME ELEMENT	Earth
ELEMENTAL CLAN	Turtle
ENERGY FLOW	Receptive
LIFE PATH	To let go and be open to the new and unknown and to spend some time outside of the usual routine, with no structure or expectations
PERSONAL GIFTS	Gregariousness, enthusiasm, idealism, determination, perseverance, respect, thoroughness, seriousness, realism
PERSONAL CHALLENGES	Skepticism, arrogance, stubbornness, authoritativeness
CORRESPONDING SEASON	Early winter—a time when nature comes to rest and to renew itself
SEASONAL ELEMENT	Air
SEASONAL TOTEM	White Buffalo
COLOR	White
PLANT	Birch tree
GEMSTONE	Quartz

SNOW GOOSE PEOPLE

The Snow Goose, a beautiful white bird with black-tipped wings, is quite gregarious, living and traveling in a large flock. Its migration pattern encompasses flying off to northern nesting grounds just as spring begins and returning with the first snows of late fall/early winter. This is a sign to Native Americans to prepare for the coming winter, an intense season requiring rest, cleansing, and renewal of the spirit. Snow geese are referred to as the "birds beyond the north winds."

Snow goose people are referred to as the "keepers of old wisdoms." They are traditional, ritualistic, and serious, sometimes appearing proper, stately, and even reserved. However, they do like to be around others, provided social gatherings are for constructive purposes as well as opportunities for exercising their intelligence.

They have a strong code of conduct and keen vision, which ensures they are meticulous and thorough in everything in which they are involved. They set high standards of performance for both themselves and others and at times can come across as overly critical and manipulative.

Snow goose people are loyal, respecting their family members, friends, and work colleagues. They can truly keep confidences and will stand by and support family, friends, and colleagues through the roughest and darkest of times.

Some Snow Goose people have a talent for storytelling. With their vivid imagination and ability to communicate clearly and concisely, they have the attributes for communicating in story form the ideals and customs that mean so much to them.

ELEMENTAL CLAN

As their birth time element is Earth, Snow Goose people belong to the Turtle clan. The turtle is one of the oldest surviving animals on earth today. It is also one of the most harmonious. Its ability to use the earth and sun for laying its eggs and hatching its young while it lives predominantly in the Water demonstrates the balance it has achieved among the elements. Like the turtle, Snow Goose people are grounded, stable and secure. They are loyal and act according to their strong values and principles. They are very practical, constructive, and industrious. Just like their element, they can be nurturing and sustaining to those around them. They will only be of value to themselves and others if they learn to accommodate the qualities of all the other elements— Fire, Air, and Water.

SEASONAL ELEMENT

Your seasonal totem animal, the White Buffalo, is closely related to the element governing the season in which you were born. For more information about your seasonal totem animal and your seasonal element, Air, see pages 48–49.

• **Strengths to cultivate** Responsibility and accountability, self-sacrifice, a sensible nature, diligence • **Possible weaknesses to address** Stubbornness, authoritative approach when dealing with others, intolerance to others' views and beliefs

TAURUS ●

BIRTH DATES: April 21 to May 20

WHO AM I?

SYMBOL	The bull Strong instincts and persevering nature
QUEST	Stability
RULING PLANET	Venus Relationships, social values, beauty/love, harmony
RULING ELEMENT	Earth Practicality, dependability, security, realism
POLARITY	Negative Receptivity, sensitivity, reserve, the desire for privacy
QUALITY	Fixed Stability, loyalty, endurance
COLOR	Pink Romantic love, empathy
FOOD	Peas, sweet potatoes, tomatoes, cardamom, apple, vanilla
FLOWER	Sweet pea, lily of the valley, rose (red)
HEALING HERB	Peppermint, tansy, thyme
GEMSTONE	Emerald Reputed to reveal the truth
SUITABLE GIFTS	Jewelry featuring emeralds, jade, or lapis lazuli; gourmet cookware; embroidery kits; or specialty garden tools

TEMPERAMENT

Taurus is the most stable sign of the zodiac and one of the most patient and determined. It is a practical, down-to-earth sign concerned with creature comforts and long-term security. Taureans have a methodical, well-planned approach to life, preferring to leave little to chance. If they believe something is worth having, they can be quite determined and focused until successful.

Like their namesake, the bull, Taureans are often handsome people, although they tend to be thickset and heavier than others in stance and facial feature. If finely formed, they, as well as their sturdier brothers and sisters under this sun sign, almost certainly will be blessed with exceptional mental and physical strength and fortitude. Overall stamina is a key characteristic of those born under the sign of Taurus.

Honest, straightforward, and open-handed (although not necessarily open-minded), Taureans make loyal and trusted friends themselves. If betrayed, however, Taureans can also turn vengeful quickly, with devastating consequences for their enemies. They can also be very critical at times. If the mood takes them, they will flex their stubborn streak and stand their ground over a small point rather than give an inch. And if Taureans do not understand something, false pride may lead them to disparage it as not worth knowing about. Many Taureans have a temper, especially if born on or around April 26. Many must fight their biggest battles with this aspect of their own nature. Personal areas that Taureans may need to develop include learning to embrace change and innovation and to be adaptable and flexible.

LOVE AND RELATIONSHIPS

With their partners, most Taureans are tender and supportive. Ideally, their partners should be similarly appreciative of the peace and beauty that Taureans almost invariably seek to create in their homes. Because Taureans are not usually very perspicacious, they will do well to find partners who are. For instance, the right partner for a Taurean is one who can gently redirect a strong and stubborn character away from poor career choices to those where talents will be realized and rewarded. Interestingly, Taureans may combine a partnership within a marriage or other personal relationship with a successful business or commercial endeavor.

Taureans will stick to a relationship as long as humanly possible. They value a happy partnership more than anything and their home is important to them, so they will do all they can to make it attractive and comfortable. They are surprisingly sociable and make friends easily, but friends are not as important to them as their family.

WORK AND BUSINESS

Productive and focused, Taureans are at their best when using their hands and providing the "muscle" behind projects to ensure their success. Taureans work hard to maintain the status quo in their chosen profession, often resisting change—particularly if it has been thrust upon them. They value organizational rules and principles and religiously follow stated policies and procedures.

Being reliable, patient, tenacious, and conscientious, they are valued as workers. Taureans can placidly work through very long hours when more mercurial temperaments would suffer mental, emotional, and physical burnout. Taurean workers are also trustworthy, determined, purposeful, systematic, detail-oriented, and highly productive. They enjoy routine and are not easily ruffled. They are the "solid achiever" type.

Many Taureans have an excellent instinct for business and a naturally sound financial sense, but they are unlikely to be impressed by the accumulation of wealth for its own sake— although they often build up quite substantial fortunes through hard work and diligence. They are not ambitious for ambition's sake, but will pursue genuine advancement.

Taureans enjoy all occupations that call for study, fine observations, accurate records, or management skills. They often become accountants or teachers. This sign also boasts a fair representation of soldiers, lawyers, editors, and navigators. Especially if born toward the later third of the sign, Taureans may be highly creative. These Taureans will be drawn to a wide range of hands-on pursuits to express their creativity and love of beauty. Exceptional cooks, gardeners, and embroiderers are often creative Taureans.

Taureans born early in the sign period (around April 21–23) may become frequent travelers either for business—perhaps as salespeople or importers—or for pleasure. But more often than not, Taureans prefer to stay close to hearth and home. They ask for nothing more than to enjoy a pleasant voyage through life. The intrigues of politics, at home and in the workplace, do not appeal to Taureans.

Financial security is a high priority, so well established and stable businesses that offer tenure and steady advancement attract Taureans. Quiet and aesthetically pleasing surroundings are also important. Taureans prefer operating alone or behind the scenes.

Museums, galleries, and anything involving flora and fauna will also suit them.

Taureans make for reluctant leaders, as they shy away from the limelight. However, they are conservative, calm, and methodical if they find themselves in leadership positions. Taureans prefer dealing with the facts and will take their time gathering and analyzing information before forming opinions and making decisions. Employees who work hard and are committed to their jobs are valued; in return, their Taurean managers are fair and patient.

BLENDING THE SYSTEMS

Taurus born in April

The Earth sign of Taurus makes April Taureans reliable, sensible, practical, and honest. They have an artistic streak and work well with their hands. The active Earth element of their Chinese sign enhances this practicality but also brings executive ability and a refusal to allow the grass to grow under their feet. The Chinese Dragon ensures they are strong and stubborn, but their delightful sense of humor and kindness ensure their popularity. Native American Beavers are known for hard work and obstinacy in the face of failure. They take their responsibilities toward their family seriously and lavish affection and attention on those they love, although they do not hesitate to argue with loved ones when they have a point to make.

Taurus born in May

The practical Earth sign of Taurus shows that May Taureans are creative, lovers of beautiful things, family people, and reliable workers. However, they tend to be fueled with stubborn determination. Their Chinese Snake sign denotes a reserved and private nature, with the inventive mind that is typical of the backroom worker. However, the Fire element adds extroversion, enterprise, and energy. In the receptive mode, this can make them talented performers with great voices. The Native American sign of the industrious Beaver of the Turtle clan rules most of this period, ensuring that May Taureans take partnerships and family relationships very seriously.

THIRTY-THREE ●

Birth numbers or personal destiny numbers are easy to calculate. Discarding all zeros, total your date, month, and year of birth and reduce that figure to one digit. For example, if you were born on June 27, 1960, number four would be your personal destiny number: 6 + 2 + 7 + 1 + 9 + 6 = 31 = 3 + 1 = 4.

WHO AM I?

GENERAL CHARACTERISTICS	Thirty-Threes are altruistic, compassionate, and intensely committed to their goals
RULING PLANET	Venus
ELEMENT	Earth
COLORS	Green, blue
GEMSTONES	Emerald

TEMPERAMENT

Those whose birth number is thirty-three exhibit many of the characteristics of Sixes. However, while Sixes generally focus on the stability and tranquility of their home life, Thirty-Threes more typically bring the same passion to their community, the world, or the entire cosmos. They seek to nurture and be of service to all. They are often compassionate to the point of oversensitivity; disharmony and suffering of all kinds can distress them, compelling them to take action.

Thirty-Threes are profoundly altruistic and are only at ease with themselves when engaged in the attempt to bring beauty, healing, and a new direction to a troubled world. While Sixes have a strong sense of self-preservation, Thirty-Threes are often too preoccupied with their goals to focus on practicalities. While committed to an ideal of the unity of body and spirit, they regularly endanger the former in the service of the latter, whether through neglect or through a willful dismissal of their bodily needs.

The weaknesses in the constitutions of Sixes—the digestive, cardiovascular and nervous systems—are, therefore, frequently magnified in Thirty-Threes. The stresses of giving of themselves so freely and being so receptive to the unhappiness of others can also cause dietary problems. Some will overeat, finding that excess weight acts as a psychological buffer against the external world, while others will go to the other extreme, eating inadequate amounts as a form of asceticism.

Despite their devotion to humanity, Thirty-Threes are often misunderstood by the majority of people around them or even thought to be incomprehensible. Their exacting standards, intense commitment to their goals, and general state of preoccupation alienate even close friends and family members at times. They are therefore inclined to feel underappreciated and alone in the world.

They may also become so convinced that their methods and aims are right that they close themselves to alternatives, becoming obstinate even in the face of evidence. Like the other master numbers, Thirty-Threes often experience a great deal of frustration at how difficult and slow the processes of change can be. When unchecked, this frustration can sometimes lead to intolerance or depression. Their passion for harmony, however, frequently comes to their aid, rebalancing their thoughts and emotions.

LOVE AND RELATIONSHIPS

Though ruled by their hearts and spirits, Thirty-Threes may often seem distant to others owing to the magnitude of the changes they wish to achieve. They do their best to give of themselves to as many friends and community members as they can, but in doing so, they can often spread their affections a little thinly. Those closest to them—partners, family, and dearest friends—must therefore reconcile themselves to a certain amount of neglect.

Thirty-Threes are unlikely to develop any degree of intimacy with anyone who is not comparably driven and inspired. Less spiritually motivated partners will soon feel isolated within a relationship with them, while more worldly individuals may become impatient with what they perceive to be Thirty-Threes' messianic tendencies.

WORK AND BUSINESS

The most rewarding areas of work for Thirty-Threes are in education, whether within the school system or in areas of large-scale cultural change such as law reform and the correction of injustice. Realizing the need for deep knowledge before effective change is possible, many Thirty-Threes enter the academic world, studying for many years before taking on educational duties. The fields to which they are naturally attracted include philosophy, psychology, medicine, and the law.

Influential and innately gifted performers, Thirty-Threes will often find that their careers involve public speaking.

THREE ●

Birth numbers or personal destiny numbers are easy to calculate. Discarding all zeros, total your date, month, and year of birth and reduce that figure to one digit. For example, if you were born on June 27, 1960, number four would be your personal destiny number: 6 + 2 + 7 + 1 + 9 + 6 = 31 = 3 + 1 = 4.

WHO AM I?

GENERAL CHARACTERISTICS	Number Three is versatile, creative, good-natured, and multitalented.
RULING PLANET	Jupiter
ELEMENT	Fire
COLORS	Lilac, mauve, purple
GEMSTONES	Amethyst

TEMPERAMENT

People born with three as their birth number are bright, enthusiastic, and infectiously optimistic. They have difficulty understanding those who do not do their best to enjoy life at all times. Threes' communication skills and quick wit rarely fail to impress, while the broad range of their interests, their social grace, and their well-developed sense of humor combine to make them popular. This suits them well, since they typically love the limelight.

Threes are highly imaginative and versatile individuals, and although they may be competitive at times, they are self-confident enough to take setbacks, and even defeat, in their stride. Though Threes' easygoing disposition prevents many of the stress-related ailments that afflict many others, their casual and self-indulgent approach to life can sometimes cause problems. Typically bons vivants, they often eat and drink more than their systems can cope with. Fatty food is frequently their downfall, and many Threes have trouble with excess weight and high cholesterol. The stress this puts on their hearts and livers is often worsened by their fondness for alcohol and caffeine.

Despite their essentially hopeful natures, Threes who feel frustrated with their lives may be prone to addictions. Impatient with their negative feelings, they may try to repress these chemically. Other medical problems that often trouble Threes include rashes, joint pain, and injuries resulting from carelessness.

Threes' exuberance is often very entertaining to others, but it can also lead them to be treated as if they were put on the planet purely for others' amusement. They are often assumed to be superficial, lightweight individuals with a great deal of style and very little substance. While this is not altogether accurate, Threes' tendency to ignore areas of life they find disturbing helps to foster this illusion.

Their love of attention may make Threes reliant on others' approval for their own self-esteem; alternatively, it may encourage egotism. Threes may also lack concentration, self-discipline, and a spiritual dimension to their lives, leaving them poorly prepared to handle crises in their lives. Their challenge is to develop more fully rounded personalities, while maintaining their natural goodwill and good humor.

LOVE AND RELATIONSHIPS

Threes are highly sociable people who are able to communicate with virtually anyone they meet. They attract friends and possible romantic partners effortlessly. Especially in their youth, however, Threes usually prefer flirtations and casual affairs to commitment. Even when they feel the need for emotional security, they may still

 treat the task of finding a partner with all the seriousness of shopping for socks. Unsurprisingly, this may lead to numerous dalliances, which are mistaken for love until the right partner is found. Often Threes find they are ideally matched with partners who have a more serious and stable disposition, offsetting their frivolous side. Having made a commitment, Threes can be more loyal than might be expected, curbing their tendency to stray through their reluctance to hurt the feelings of someone who loves and trusts them.

WORK AND BUSINESS

Since Threes generally prefer to make a living from their creativity, many are attracted to the arts. Some have the self-discipline for the more isolating art forms such as writing or painting, but the majority prefer careers where they can mix with others or, better still, perform. Consequently, a number of Threes become actors, dancers, musicians, and, given their effortless wit, comedians.

Other Threes use their talent for communication in sales, advertising, lecturing, or journalism. Although fairly well suited to working in groups, Threes are particularly uncomfortable when overlooked and resent any form of interference in their jobs.

TIGER ●

YEAR OF BIRTH: 1914, 1926, 1938, 1950, 1962, 1974, 1986, 1998, 2010

WHO AM I?

NATURAL ENERGY	Yang
NATURAL ELEMENT	Wood
CORRESPONDING TIME	(Tiger ascendant) 3 A.M.–5 A.M.
CORRESPONDING MONTH	February
CORRESPONDING DIRECTION	East/Northeast
CORRESPONDING SEASON	Early spring
CHARACTER TRAITS	Charismatic, bold, protective, generous, curious, lucky, courageous, optimistic, idealistic, determined, intelligent, sensitive, benevolent, ambitious, loyal, honorable, reckless
PERSONAL NEEDS	Tigers need to relax and be pampered, and they need to be persuaded to take time out occasionally from their hectic lifestyles.
LIFE CHALLENGES	To appreciate patience and heed the wise counsel of others

TEMPERAMENT

Tigers have a magnetic, uplifting, motivating presence, and many of the qualities of good leaders. Tiger people are born adventurers and optimistic daredevils. Full of excited expectation, they know only two speeds: full speed or ground to a halt. They live for the moment, engaging in life passionately and with childlike excitement. Generally lucky, most Tigers are able to triumph over all types of misadventure. They demand plenty of space in their relationships and as few rules as possible in their daily lives. Only in retirement do they start to settle down and find some peace and contentment.

LOVE AND RELATIONSHIPS

Blessed with a sunny disposition and opposed to wallowing in the negative, Tigers are extremely supportive and uplifting to friends who suffer from ill health or bad times. They love having a busy social life and cannot resist the allure of parties. Gifted storytellers, they are a must at any social gathering, and they love to dress up.

Tigers are extremely protective and generous with their loved ones. They are often seen as childish because of their engaging presence and energetic approach to life. They are wonderfully natural, inspiring, and encouraging with children, and are often the favorite aunt or uncle. Tigers make great parents themselves, provided they can balance their time with the children with time away from the family home.

Tigers are the courageous and passionate lovers of the Chinese zodiac. Full of zest and personal charisma, they romp from one romance to another, never quite satisfied, and on the lookout for someone unusual or different. Ruled by their hearts, they follow their instincts when it comes to romance. Attraction to adventure and the unusual will keep many Tigers single until well into middle age.

WORK AND BUSINESS

Tigers' key strengths in the workplace are their infectious motivation and enthusiasm. With their keen sense of urgency, they like to get things done quickly. They make formidable business leaders who can quickly rise to high positions, provided they follow the wise counsel of those they trust. Their loyalty and compassion for their colleagues will ensure their popularity spills over from their social to their professional lives. Their honesty and desire to protect the less fortunate will often see them take up many causes; they deplore workplace injustice. Ideal occupations for Tigers include entrepreneur, actor, writer, union leader, explorer, teacher, or military leader.

In Chinese astrology, each of the five elements—Metal, Water, Wood , Fire, and Earth—is dominant in a particular year. This imbues the animal associated with each year with a particular character.

- If you were born in 1914 or 1974, you are a **WOOD TIGER**.
- If you were born in 1926 or 1986, you are a **FIRE TIGER**.
- If you were born in 1938 or 1998, you are an **EARTH TIGER**.
- If you were born in 1950 or 2010, you are a **METAL TIGER**.
- If you were born in 1962, you are a **WATER TIGER**.

TWENTY-TWO ●

Birth numbers or personal destiny numbers are easy to calculate. Discarding all zeros, total your date, month, and year of birth and reduce that figure to one digit. For example, if you were born on June 27, 1960, number four would be your personal destiny number: 6 + 2 + 7 + 1 + 9 + 6 = 31 = 3 + 1 = 4.

WHO AM I?

GENERAL CHARACTERISTICS	Number Twenty-Two has high ideals and goals, and is highly psychic.
RULING PLANET	Uranus
ELEMENT	Air
COLORS	Blue, gray
GEMSTONES	Sapphire

TEMPERAMENT

Like elevens, those whose birth number is twenty-two are highly visionary individuals who often influence others. However, since twenty-two can be reduced numerologically to four, the practicality associated with that number also affects them. This makes Twenty-Twos more effective than elevens at putting their ideas into action instead of just inspiring others to do so.

Twenty-Twos are extremely ambitious people who feel driven to achieving change on a global scale. They have the self-confidence and optimism to take on the most daunting problems, the imagination and intellectual skills to formulate solutions, and the pragmatism to carry them out.

While Twenty-Twos' compulsive work ethic often takes its toll physically, they share some of the stability and security consciousness of fours and this often prevents them from being entirely neglectful of their health. Aware of their habit of using food, caffeine, alcohol, and other substances to energize or relax themselves, they can usually ensure this does not get out of hand. However, when their projects are not going as well or as quickly as they desire, their bodies do tend to suffer from the effects of overindulgence.

Driven by their aspirations, many Twenty-Twos are afflicted with stress-related ailments, such as headaches, muscular strain and constipation, often from a very early age. They can also be extremely careless of their safety when preoccupied.

While enjoying the fact that they are in the forefront of their field, Twenty-Twos often feel alone and rather alienated from others. Their emotional remoteness often means that, despite their desire to benefit humanity, Twenty-Twos can be quite tactless, impatient, and domineering. They often believe the ends justify the means, and are prepared to ride roughshod over anyone who gets in their way.

Twenty-Twos are prone to intolerance in the face of disagreement, disorder, and the failure of others to carry out their instructions efficiently. They are also exasperated when their associates do not display the same intensity about their shared goals. They must also guard against pessimism when their progress is impeded and against depression and listlessness once their goal has been reached.

LOVE AND RELATIONSHIPS

Charismatic and energetic, Twenty-Twos attract many admirers, but many people find their intensity intimidating. For this reason, they may have fewer intimate friends than most people do. Those who do get close to them, however, usually have very strong characters themselves and are very loyal.

Twenty-Twos are rarely romantic, but they value the love and support of their partners highly. They may neglect to mention this,

though, as their minds are often focused on grand schemes rather than on individuals. As natural leaders, they can sometimes dominate their partners and attempt to control every aspect of their lives. Consequently, their

partners are usually either very docile or very assertive and self-confident. Those who are neither tend to give up on the relationship after a fairly short time.

WORK AND BUSINESS

For Twenty-Twos, work should be fulfilling and allow them to realize their ambitions. If it is neither of those things, they may experience great frustration while occupying the positions they need in order to put their epic plans into action. Once they are in a position of leadership, their aversion to disorder makes them exceptional organizers; their understanding that great achievements often require the united efforts of many individuals makes them ideally suited to coordinating and maintaining groups of workers— or even entire companies. Being agents of global change, many Twenty-Twos are drawn to politics, the law, human rights organizations, ecology, or religious and spiritual movements.

TWO ●

Birth numbers or personal destiny numbers are easy to calculate. Discarding all zeros, total your date, month, and year of birth and reduce that figure to one digit. For example, if you were born on June 27, 1960, number four would be your personal destiny number: 6 + 2 + 7 + 1 + 9 + 6 = 31 = 3 + 1 = 4.

WHO AM I?

GENERAL CHARACTERISTICS	Number Two is kind and gentle and has an approachable nature.
RULING PLANET	Moon
ELEMENT	Water
COLORS	Cream, green
GEMSTONES	Jade, pearl, moonstone

TEMPERAMENT

Those whose birth number is two are gentle, amiable people who place a very high value on harmony and peace. Their partners, families and friends are of primary importance to them and are showered with affection, support, and nurturing by the naturally generous Twos. They love socializing and their sense of balance allows them to be both entertaining conversationalists and extremely good listeners.

Twos enjoy being able to help others with their problems and often intuitively come up with perfect solutions. Since they find it easy to see both sides of any dispute, they are excellent at reconciliation. The nurturing skills of Twos often extend to taking care of themselves. Seeking harmony in all things, they typically eat a well-balanced diet and include a sensible amount of exercise into their routines. Many instinctively chose their foods to harmonize with the seasons and prefer small regular meals rather than feasts.

Twos' emotional sensitivity can, however, throw them badly out of kilter. Their well-being is often governed by the quality of their relationships, and emotional setbacks and loss can often send them spiraling into depression. This may result in overeating, anorexia, addictions, or bipolar disorders. Twos need to be conscious of this tendency and to rebalance their periodic unhappiness by seeking consolation in their friends and through calming techniques such as yoga and meditation.

Twos rely heavily on the good opinions of others, making them reluctant to do anything that might jeopardize their popularity. Although they realize this makes them seem weak-willed, they usually prefer this to being considered troublesome or foolish. This overcautious approach to life can turn the simplest decision into a major problem for Twos, and their constant overanalysis of every aspect of a choice frequently results in missed opportunities or greatly delayed progress.

To maintain the approval of others, Twos will often deny their personal desires, causing resentment that will flare up in situations that have little connection to the cause, or they may descend into a sustained sulk. The challenge for Twos is to strengthen both their emotional defenses and their spirit of independence.

LOVE AND RELATIONSHIPS

Twos' obliging and affable personalities attract countless friends who benefit greatly from their encouragement, advice, and consideration. Though some Twos may be somewhat shy in unfamiliar company, their warmth is quickly recognized and bonds are soon forged. They have slightly more trouble forming romances, rarely feeling confident enough to make the first move. However, once they are aware of a possible partner's interest in them, their appetite for affection rapidly banishes their timidity.

While Twos are very attentive, loving, and supportive in their relationships, they have an equal appetite for these qualities themselves and become despondent if neglected. They can also be overly vulnerable to criticism, whether real or imagined, and have few skills at coping with the loss of a partner or the failure of a marriage.

WORK AND BUSINESS

Twos prefer working in a team far more than working in isolation. Though they are usually multitalented, their versatility rarely extends to leadership, the mere idea of which can make them feel nervous. They can, however, be very effective in middle management since they not only work well with a wide range of people but are also skilled at helping them interact efficiently and harmoniously.

They are talented negotiators and are very well suited to positions in public relations, diplomacy, counseling, and psychiatry. Their fair-mindedness and interest in justice may attract them to the law, but their aversion to arguments means they should consider becoming academic, rather than practicing, lawyers.

VIRGO

BIRTH DATES: August 23 to September 22

WHO AM I?

SYMBOL	*The Virgin or Maiden* *Virgo's drive for perfection and veiled sensuality*
QUEST	*Analysis*
RULING PLANET	*Mercury* *Communication, intellectual ability, decision-making*
RULING ELEMENT	*Earth* *Practicality, dependability, security, realism*
POLARITY	*Negative* *Receptivity, sensitivity, reserve, the desire for privacy*
QUALITY	*Mutable* *Adaptability, flexibility, cohesiveness*
COLOR	*Brown* *Symbolizing the soil of earth and promising good fortune through stability*
FOOD	*Beans, celery, caraway, dill, marjoram*
FLOWER	*Poppy, aster, lily of the valley*
HEALING HERB	*Fennel, lavender, valerian* *Fennel is useful for infusing the Virgoan soul with courage.*
GEMSTONE	*Sapphire* *Nobility, virtue, justice, loyalty*
SUITABLE GIFTS	*Jewelry featuring sapphires or adventurine; small antique collectibles; fine art for the home; and classical music recordings*

TEMPERAMENT

Virgo is the calmest sign of the zodiac. Sensible and meticulous, Virgoans win the respect of the other, less focused signs. Practical and analytical and able to categorize large amounts of information, they have razor-sharp perception and probing minds. They offer improved efficiency and effectiveness, but their drive for perfectionism can breed narrow-mindedness and fussiness.

The Virgoan urge to create perfection reflects the innate creativity of people born under this sign, their keen sense of aesthetics and order, and their natural predilection for the worthwhile in life. From a very early age, they are often interested in the visual and decorative arts and crafts, antiques, and fine music.

Virgoans born toward the middle of the sign, from August 30 to September 5, often possess psychic powers. These may manifest as a distinct occult ability or a talent for readily assessing both the best and the worst characteristics of other people.

Those born toward the end of the sign, from around September 9 onward, can be quite complicated individuals, combining a quixotic nature and a hasty temper with the more typical Virgoan eye for detail and highly retentive memory.

Personal areas Virgoans may wish to develop include accepting that "to err is human," setting realistic expectations, and learning to say no.

LOVE AND FRIENDSHIP

Virgoans have few important relationships, but they are intensely loyal to those who matter to them. They prefer to show their love by doing things for their partners rather than by simply being affectionate.

Virgoans thrive in relationships when their partners unfailingly demonstrate total faith in their professional abilities. Those born under this sign are well matched also with jolly, happy-go-lucky partners who can encourage them to relax. Learning how to play, to rediscover the joy and spontaneity of childhood, is of vital importance to Virgoans, for their tendency to work far too hard means they may turn even their hobbies into work.

Kindly, protective, capable partners are ideal supports for Virgoans, who typically are not particularly strong and can often overtax themselves. When stressed in any way, the Virgoan tendency to be impossibly finicky and fussy, intolerant, and critical of anything less than perfection often becomes more marked. Those born under this sign also tend to worry unnecessarily about health. Partners who can help Virgoans to keep their stress levels manageable are a boon to the partnership.

Virgoans can also become immersed in their own ambitions, so much so that they may appear to neglect family and friends while working themselves to exhaustion. They are well complemented by emotionally secure partners who will not feel hurt or abandoned when the Virgoan focuses almost obsessively on work and career.

WORK AND BUSINESS

At work, Virgoans come across as efficient, methodical, astute, and logical. They put their heads down and bury themselves in the details of their tasks, with little awareness of the interpersonal aspects of office life. They set very high standards for themselves. This can be stressful for them—unless they receive regular feedback on their efforts and performance. Their perfectionism underlies their methodical approach to work and their gift for detail and accuracy. They tend to have quite exceptional memories and do well in tests involving mental calculation or factual recall. They usually make good students, historians, navigators, health practitioners, and scientists. Being attuned to mental rather than physical jobs, Virgoans love to  work with ideas and with words. They are also keen and shrewd, which will stand them in good stead if they follow careers in journalism—often particularly suited to those born toward the beginning of the sign, from August 23 to August 26.

Virgoans are renowned for creating tranquil conditions around them, whether at work or at home. They often gravitate toward work linked with peacemaking and humanitarian issues, acting as go-betweens, arbitrators, diplomats, and even missionaries. However, Virgoans typically work very hard, so that while working for the betterment of others, they may simultaneously overlook their own well-being. In Virgoans born on August 27, this capacity for hard work can coexist with a quirky, imaginative nature. These are the Virgoans who are likely to come up with a creative and challenging idea and then methodically complete each task necessary for realizing it. Of all the birth dates in the zodiac, August 27 is the one that nearly always produces an extremely interesting temperament. It is the birthday of the person most likely to invent something or suddenly demonstrate a previously hidden talent.

The Virgoan's methodical nature also favors work that involves planning and periodic checking. Virgoans are happy to accept responsibility, so careers requiring assiduous supervision and inspection, such as editing, pharmacy, banking, insurance, and product management are indicated for them.

Virgoans prefer order and structure. An office environment, library, or science laboratory is the ideal workplace. They need to feel useful and are happiest when providing support to others or identifying and fixing problems. Virgoans do not operate well in isolation or in a constantly changing environment. Virgoans' talents do not lend themselves naturally to the leadership role, unless it is the operations or finance side of a business that is being managed. Virgo bosses can be openly critical and sticklers for rules and regulations. They expect punctuality, attention to detail, and efficiency from their staff. In return, they are good at clarifying responsibilities, providing clear direction, and prioritizing work.

BLENDING THE SYSTEMS

Virgoans born in August

The practical and intellectual Earth sign of Virgo denotes literary and communication skills as well as a talent for research and an eye for detail, but also the perfectionist's tendency to worry about insignificant details. The Chinese sign of the active Metal Monkey adds independence, strength, common sense, commercial ability, and a talent for getting jobs done. There are times when August Virgoans may work far too hard for their own good. The Native American sign of the Brown Bear of the Turtle clan gives them a cheerful nature and an excellent sense of humor, and makes them eager to discover as much as possible about everything. The only real drawback is a tendency to take on lame ducks or to try to rescue those who are beyond help.

Virgoans born in September

September Virgoans have quick minds and a talent for research and analysis, but this can make them too concerned with details. Their Chinese astrology receptive Metal element adds ambition and an innovative mind, and it draws them toward the world of show business and the arts. The sign of the Rooster adds honesty as well as glamour, but it also means these Virgoans have a tendency to brag about their achievements. Their Native American Brown Bear of the Turtle clan signifies intelligence, curiosity, a realistic attitude, and a sense of humor.

WATER

Dominant element in Chinese Astrology
YEARS OF BIRTH: 1902, 1903, 1912, 1913, 1922, 1923, 1932, 1933, 1942, 1943, 1952, 1953, 1962, 1963, 1972, 1973, 1982, 1983, 1992, 1993, 2012, 2013

WHO AM I?

1912, 1972 • THE WATER RAT

Double Water: Intuition, communication, and emotions Double Water lends these Rats a natural eloquence, leading them into communication-centered careers such as public speaking or professional writing.

1913, 1973 • THE WATER OX

Water controlled by Earth: Emotional accessibility This is just what Oxen need—access to their emotional side. Water Oxen are softer and more approachable than other Oxen. Empathetic and considerate, they are still sufficiently practical.

1902, 1962 • THE WATER TIGER

From Water grows Wood : An enhancing combination Water makes Tigers quieter and more carefree. Water Tigers are highly intuitive. Socially, they have an extroverted, optimistic presence. Water Tigers are sensitive to others' needs.

1903, 1963 • THE WATER RABBIT

From Water grows Wood : An enhancing combination Water Rabbits are supersensitive, acutely aware of themselves in all environments. This can create a neurotic, inwardly focused personality.

1952, 2012 • THE WATER DRAGON

Water is directed by Earth: Empathy and intuition Dragons need a dose of Water to soften their exuberant personalities and occasionally shift their focus from themselves. Water Dragons are far more considerate and caring than other dragons.

1953, 2013 • THE WATER SNAKE

Fire is controlled by Water: Clarity and intuition Water Snakes are amazingly gifted—the embodiment of intuitive perception. With their keen sensory acuity, little passes them by. Water Snakes are often found in spiritual professions, where they can utilize their gifts to see beyond the obvious.

1942, 2002 • THE WATER HORSE

Fire is controlled by Water: Intuition and mental creativity Water Horses have less focus on their physical world and have creative and/or communication skills. They are often gifted orators, able to build a story to an emotional finale.

1943, 2003 • THE WATER SHEEP

Water is controlled by Earth: Emotions and intuition Water Sheep engage with life emotionally, rarely using logic or reflection for objectivity. They are easily wounded by criticism and extremely sensitive to their surroundings. Their mental health and physical state are accordingly delicate.

1932, 1992 • WATER MONKEY

From Metal comes Water: Empathy and reflection Water ensures that these Monkeys are not too quick to trifle with others' feelings. Water Monkeys demonstrate empathy and will use their keen intellects to solve problems rather than creating them. They are group-oriented rather than individually motivated.

1933, 1993 • WATER ROOSTER

From Metal comes Water: Empathy and intuition Water Roosters are softer and more flexible than other roosters. They use their intuition to avoid being too direct with others. With their appealing combination of self-awareness, flamboyance, and understanding of others, they are the focus of attention.

1922, 1982 • WATER DOG

From Metal comes Water: Empathy Water Dogs are more reflective and adaptable than other Dogs. They are more lenient on themselves and others and will allow for much fun and frivolity in their lives. They will also fall for any sad-luck story. Water Dogs are popular with others and will never want for love, friendship, or support, as they are more prone than other Dogs to acceptance and to giving unconditional love.

1923, 1983 • WATER PIG

Double Water: Intuition, communication, and emotions Double Water intensifies the pig's already emotionally charged personality, making Water Pigs supersensitive to others and overly indulgent. Increasingly introspective with age and experience, Water Pigs' ability to deal with hardships in life can quickly diminish.

WATER

In the Native American belief system, Fire, Water, Air, and Earth are the four elements considered the most important natural forces. They permeate every aspect of life, ensuring that living things go through a recurring process of birth, life, death, and regeneration. The different elements also cause differences in personality, highlighting particular strengths and weaknesses of character. The elements are also the foundation of many other aspects of the natural world. The following table outlines the correspondences of Water.

WHO AM I?

KEY ATTRIBUTES	Sensitivity, flexibility, intuition, creativity, communication
AREAS GOVERNED BY THE ELEMENT	The soul, emotions
SEASON OF LIFE IT GOVERNS	Summer
DIRECTION	South
TIME OF DAY IT GOVERNS	Midday
TIME OF LIFE IT GOVERNS	Adulthood (18–40 years)
ANIMAL BIRTH TOTEM	Snake: 10/23–11/21 (N); 4/20–5/20 (S) Wolf: 2/19–3/20 (N); 8/23–22/9 (S) Woodpecker: 6/21–7/22 (N); 12/22–1/19 (S)
ANIMAL SEASONAL TOTEM	Brown Bear, Salmon, Woodpecker

We are all affected by two elements influencing our character and behavior at any one time—the element of the birth time animal totem and the element of the seasonal animal totem. If the two elements and their key attributes are taken into account when analyzing each animal totem's character, a more detailed and accurate description of that totem will be gained.

WATER AS BIRTH TIME ELEMENT

The instinctive behavior of each birth time animal totem is influenced by the birth time element. It is this element that creates the foundation of each animal totem's basic nature—the essence of who you are. Animal totems with Water as their birth time element are the Snake (see pages 154–155), Wolf (see pages 180–181), and Woodpecker (see pages 184–185).

With Water as their birth time element, these animal totems are emotionally sensitive and flexible. They operate by using their communication skills and their intuition, which is usually well developed. They are empathetic and creative.

WATER AS SEASONAL ELEMENT

The seasonal animal totem provides additional gifts and qualities. These qualities relate to the totems' inner senses, spiritual endeavors, and general behavior. The animal totems with Earth as their seasonal element are the Brown Bear, Salmon, and Woodpecker. These summer animal totems have the force of Water directing their general behavior. People born during this time of the year therefore tend to act with sensitivity toward others. They have flexible and creative natures, and their communication skills are generally well developed.

People born during summer all have the coyote as their seasonal totem. They often experience rapid growth—physically, mentally, emotionally, and spiritually. They are most productive in the heat of the day (midday), when their sharp senses can be utilized and their newly developed maturity well tested. They represent the human lifetime of young adulthood, approximately eighteen to forty years of age.

The summertime animal totem is the Coyote. Coyotes are wild and cunning animals that have so far proved adaptable to the encroachment of civilization on their natural terrain. They use their agility and sharp senses to avoid unnecessary contact with humans.

PURE SIGN

Pure signs occur when the season and birth time elements are the same. The Woodpecker is the pure Water sign (Water of Water). People with the Woodpecker totem demonstrate highly refined

intuition and creativity. With their very flexible and intuitive natures, they are the supreme communicators. With so much flexibility and creativity, Woodpecker people, more than any other sign, need to take a stand on their personal convictions and principles. They should learn to take decisive action to realize their ideas. They also need to approach their everyday activities in a methodical fashion so that these activities can bear fruit for the benefit of all.

WOLF

BIRTH DATES: Northern Hemisphere: February 19 to March 20
Southern Hemisphere: August 23 to September 22

WHO AM I?

BIRTH TIME ANIMAL TOTEM	Wolf
BIRTH TIME ELEMENT	Water
ELEMENTAL CLAN	Frog
ENERGY FLOW	Receptive
LIFE PATH	To harness the emotional winds that can buffet you in many different physical directions, and make you subject to many different moods
PERSONAL GIFTS	Creativity, intuitiveness, trustworthiness, loyalty, philosophical nature, spirituality, genuineness, selflessness
PERSONAL CHALLENGES	Restlessness, depression, nervousness, indecisiveness
CORRESPONDING SEASON	Late winter—a time of big, strong, blustery winds
SEASONAL ELEMENT	Air
SEASONAL TOTEM	White Buffalo
COLOR	Blue-green
PLANT	Plantain
GEMSTONE	Turquoise

WOLF PEOPLE

Native Americans admire the wolf, seeing it as a fine example of the successful integration of individualism and family unity. Wolves live in family packs in which clearly defined roles are respected, yet they will also strike out on their own, exploring new terrain for a while before returning to the pack. Witnessing a wolf howling at the moon is a message to turn within and seek harmony.

Wolf people are prone to contradictions in their characters. For instance, they may become restless if little or no individual space and freedom are provided. They may also become stressed and worried if left on their own for too long. It is a constant tug-of-war that wolf people impose on themselves, a struggle between freedom and independence, and home and security. This struggle is characterized by the season of their birth—late winter is a time of big, blustery winds.

Among some of the gifts Wolf people possess are their highly tuned senses. Their sharp instincts and keen sense of their environment and the people around them enable them to pick up messages very swiftly. If something or someone does not feel right, wolf people will quickly back away, often without being able to tell what it is that is making them feel uneasy.

Wolves are sensitive and can easily take offense, being hurt by the actions and words of others. This is particularly evident in their love life, which can be rocky at times. They need to temper this by seeking clarification and confirmation of others' intentions and by trying to control their own reactions more carefully.

ELEMENTAL CLAN

As their birth time element is Water, wolves belong to the Frog clan. The frog is a very distinctive and adaptable creature. Its body is slick and nimble, and this gives it much agility and flexibility. The metamorphosis from tadpole to adult frog demonstrates its ability to transform itself. Like the frog, Wolf people are very flexible and emotionally fluid individuals who possess the ability to transform themselves to suit their environments. The Water element provides them with creativity and expressiveness, making them skilled communicators. Just like Water, Frog clan members' creativity can shift from stagnant pools and dams to rushing tides and pounding waves. Their ideas and innovations have the capacity to transform people and environments, provided they can set clear directions for themselves and apply the discipline required for reaching their goals.

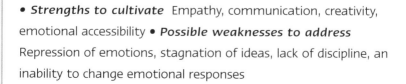

SEASONAL ELEMENT

Your seasonal totem animal, the White Buffalo, is closely related to the element governing the season in which you were born. For more information about your seasonal totem animal and your seasonal element, Air, see pages 178–79.

• **Strengths to cultivate** Empathy, communication, creativity, emotional accessibility • **Possible weaknesses to address** Repression of emotions, stagnation of ideas, lack of discipline, an inability to change emotional responses

WOOD ●

Dominant Element in Chinese Astrology
YEARS OF BIRTH: 1914, 1915, 1924, 1925, 1934, 1935, 1944, 1955, 1964, 1965, 1974, 1975, 1984, 1985, 1994, 1995, 2004, 2005

WHO AM I?

1924, 1984 • WOOD RAT

From Water grows Wood: An enhancing combination Wood Rats display more creative talent and interest in spirituality than other Rats. Their optimism and heightened resourcefulness overcome much of the Rat's usual worries about security, and this frees them to indulge a little in their passions. Caring and empathetic, Wood Rats are popular.

1925, 1985 • WOOD OX

Earth is controlled by Wood: Harnessed strengths Wood Oxen are dependable and stable, clear of purpose, and rigid adherents to their principles and values. Highly ethical, they avoid the lightweight and lighthearted. They tend to follow a traditional path, enjoying the comfort and security of a home and family.

1914, 1974 • WOOD TIGER

Double Wood: Expansion and personal growth Double Wood gives the Tiger twice as much gaiety and childlike enthusiasm. Wood Tigers are irrepressible and will often be surrounded by an adoring crowd. They detest commitment in all forms, preferring to spend their time traveling, exploring, learning, and generally experiencing all that life has to offer.

1915, 1975 • WOOD RABBIT

Double Wood: Expansion and personal growth Wood Rabbits are usually artistically talented and have creative occupations. They are quite generous and give freely of themselves. While eager for financial wealth, they are quick spenders, particularly when it comes to traveling for inspiration.

1964, 2024 • WOOD DRAGON

Earth is utilized by Wood: Harnessed strengths Wood Dragons are generally creative, engaging, and beautiful to behold, full of elegance, style, and refined taste. As such, they are naturals in the highest social circles. They usually marry well and spend their time directing public charity events.

1965, 2025 • WOOD SNAKE

Wood fuels Fire: Sensuality and sexuality Wood Snakes may give in to laziness and indulgence in sensual delights rather than accomplishing anything outside of their own needs. Career, power, and influence are not as important to Wood Snakes as they are to other Snakes, so they can fall far short of their true potential.

1954, 2014 • WOOD HORSE

Fire is controlled by Water: Recklessness tamed Wood Horses are more relaxed and less excitable than other Horses. They demonstrate stability in all facets of life, from romance to career. Wood Horses are cooperative and caring and tend to be gullible.

1955, 2015 • WOOD SHEEP

Earth controls Wood: Stability and direction Wood Sheep are extremely creative and artistic. Unmotivated by money or fame, they spend all their time on creative and artistic pursuits. Generous to a fault, Wood Sheep are compassionate and caring.

1944, 2004 • WOOD MONKEY

Wood is controlled by Metal: Strength and domination Wood Monkeys are more balanced and less volatile than other Monkeys, with a methodical approach to solving problems. These Monkeys are more capable of specific achievements and less attracted to practical jokes.

1945, 2005 • WOOD ROOSTER

Wood is controlled by Metal: Expansion Wood Roosters show an early interest in personal growth and take every opportunity to challenge their own beliefs and explore other options. They are enthusiastic seekers of knowledge and their homes are full of half-read books. Wood Roosters are more flexible and adaptable than other Roosters.

1934, 1994 • WOOD DOG

Earth is utilized by Wood: Personal growth Wood Dogs are more fun loving and optimistic than other Dogs. They are open to life's experiences, willing to change their values and principles. Wood Dogs, deeply empathetic, place fewer expectations on themselves.

1935, 1955 • WOOD PIG

From Water grows Wood: Enhancing combination Wood gives Pigs the opportunity for total self-expression. Wood Pigs can talk and talk and talk. They need to consider careers where their verbal talents can be appreciated. Wood Pigs can be too quick to express their opinions and need to avoid consciously offending others.

WOODPECKER

BIRTH DATES: Northern Hemisphere: June 21 to July 22

Southern Hemisphere: December 22 to January 19

WHO AM I?

BIRTH TIME ANIMAL TOTEM	Woodpecker
BIRTH TIME ELEMENT	Water
ELEMENTAL CLAN	Frog
ENERGY FLOW	Receptive
LIFE PATH	To take time out each day to love and nurture yourself as much as you do others and to stay true to yourself and to what you feel is right
PERSONAL GIFTS	Intuition, loving nature, generosity, sensitivity, trust, devotion, loyalty, calmness
PERSONAL CHALLENGES	Vulnerability, insecurity, gullibility, anxiety
CORRESPONDING SEASON	Early summer—a time of long, hot days
SEASONAL ELEMENT	Water
SEASONAL TOTEM	Coyote
COLOR	Pink
PLANT	Wild rose
GEMSTONE	Carnelian

WOODPECKER PEOPLE

Native Americans respect Woodpeckers for their unique drumming behavior, as this is seen to represent the beating of the heart. Hearing a Woodpecker play its song out loud to the world is a sign to Native Americans to tune into their own heartsong and courageously follow its message.

Woodpecker people live their lives according to what they feel is right. They listen to their hearts rather than their minds, thus avoiding an overly logical approach to decision-making.

Woodpeckers are seen as the most nurturing, charitable, and generous of all people. They are blessed with naturally strong principles and values, to which they adhere in their everyday lives. They have an open mind about everyone they meet and an open heart for all. They are neither discriminatory nor distrusting.

To Woodpeckers, the whole world is just one large extended family. They are particularly home-oriented. They highly value their relationships with others. As family and friends mean a lot to Woodpeckers, they take their commitments seriously, generously opening their homes and giving of themselves and what they possess to ease the hardships of others. Woodpeckers thrive when in the company of others.

With all of these qualities, Woodpeckers are naturally intuitive and sensitive to their environment and those around them. They are particularly good in a crisis, when their calm and caring approach is much appreciated.

ELEMENTAL CLAN

As their birth time element is Water, Woodpeckers belong to the Frog clan. The frog is a very distinctive and adaptable creature. Its body is slick and nimble, and this gives it much agility and flexibility. Its signature "croak" is a serenade to many, and the metamorphosis from tadpole to adult frog demonstrates its ability to transform itself. Like the frog, Woodpecker people are very flexible and emotionally fluid individuals who possess the ability to transform themselves to suit their environments. The Water element provides them with creativity and expressiveness, making them skilled communicators. Just like Water, Frog clan members' creativity can shift from stagnant pools and dams to rushing tides and pounding waves. Their ideas and innovations have the capacity to transform people and environments, provided they can set clear directions for themselves and apply the discipline required for reaching their goals.

SEASONAL ELEMENT

Your seasonal totem animal, the coyote, is closely related to the element governing the season in which you were born. For more information about your seasonal totem animal and your seasonal element, Water, see pages 178–179.

• **Strengths to cultivate** Empathy, communication, creativity, emotional accessibility • **Possible weaknesses to address** Repression of emotions, stagnation of ideas, lack of discipline, an inability to change emotional responses

GLOSSARY

ACTIVE ENERGY In Chinese astrology, like yang energy. In animal totem astrology, this energy is associated with the Sun and conscious activity. It is also linked to the elements of Fire and Air. The animal totems with either Fire or Air as their birth time element demonstrate active energy in their general behavior.

ANIMAL SIGN In Chinese astrology, one of 12 animals that rule the year, month and time of a person's birth. They are the Rat, Ox, Tiger, Rabbit, Dragon, Snake, Horse, Sheep, Monkey, Rooster, Dog, and Pig. In animal totem astrology, another set of 12 animals are believed to rule the time, day and season of a person's birth. They are the Snow Goose, Otter, Wolf, Hawk, Beaver, Deer, Woodpecker, Salmon, Brown Bear, Raven, Snake, and Owl.

ANIMAL TOTEM In animal totem astrology, an animal symbol representing a birth time, seasonal, or elemental clan totem.

ASCENDANT In Chinese astrology, the animal sign ruling the time of birth.

ASTROLOGY A form of divination based on the position of the planets, moon, and sun at the time of a person's birth.

BIRTH TIME ELEMENT In animal totem astrology, the element of nature ruling a person's time of birth.

BIRTH TIME TOTEM ANIMAL In animal totem astrology, an animal representing a person's time of birth.

CARDINAL SIGN See Quality.

DOMINANT ANIMAL OR SIGN In Chinese astrology, the animal ruling the year of birth.

DOMINANT ELEMENT In Chinese astrology, the element of nature ruling the year of birth.

ELEMENTS Natural energies or forces that indicate nature's influence on the astrological signs of various systems. In the Western and animal totem systems, these elements are Earth, Air, Fire, and Water; in Chinese astrology they are Metal, Water, Wood, Fire, and Earth.

ELEMENTAL CLAN In animal totem astrology, this is the animal group a person belongs to, given that person's birth time element.

ENERGY FLOW   In animal totem astrology, energy flows through life in two complementary ways: actively and receptively. It is the flow of energy that gives force to the elements of Earth, Fire, Air, and Water. Each birth and seasonal totem has either an active or a receptive energy flow.

FIXED SIGN   See Quality.

LOVE SIGN   In Chinese astrology, the animal sign ruling the month of birth.

MUTABLE SIGN   See Quality.

NATIVE AMERICANS   The earliest human inhabitants of North America.

NATURAL ELEMENT   In Chinese astrology, this refers to the element normally associated with each animal sign.

PURE SIGN   In Chinese astrology, this occurs when the same animal sign rules both the year and time of birth. In animal totem astrology, a pure sign occurs when the same element rules the time of birth and the season.

QUALITY   In Western astrology, this refers to the groups of signs that can be classified as cardinal, fixed or mutable. Cardinal signs are enterprising individuals, fixed signs uphold the status quo, and mutable signs bring change and closure.

RECEPTIVE ENERGY   In Chinese astrology, this is like yin energy. In animal totem astrology, this energy is associated with the Moon and unconscious activity, and is linked to the elements of Earth and Water. Animal totems with either Earth or Water as the corresponding element as their birth time element demonstrate receptive energy in their general behavior.

SEASONAL ELEMENT   In animal totem astrology, the element ruling the season in which a person is born; sometimes referred to as the "principal element."

SEASONAL TOTEM ANIMAL   In animal totem astrology, the animal totem representing the season in which a person is born; sometimes referred to as the "directional totem."

YANG ENERGY   In Chinese astrology, yang energy is extrovert, positive, or masculine energy.

YIN ENERGY   In Chinese astrology, yin energy is introvert, negative, or feminine energy.

INDEX

Thunder Bay Press
An imprint of the Advantage Publishers Group
5880 Oberlin Drive, San Diego, CA 92121-4794
www.thunderbaybooks.com

With grateful acknowledgment to Debbie Burns for reproduction of a portion of her works *Animal Totem Astrology* and *Chinese Horoscopes*, and to Sasha Fenton for reproduction of a portion of her work *Astrology: A Guide to Eastern and Western Horoscopes*.

ISBN 1-59223-289-2
Library of Congress Cataloging-in-Publication Data available on request.

Set in Birka and LT Ergo on QuarkXPress
Printed in Singapore by Tien Wah Press (Pte) Ltd
1 2 3 4 5   09 08 07 06 05